## KOLBE: A SAINT IN AUSCHWITZ

Desmond Forristal is a native of Dublin. He was ordained priest in 1955 and has served in several parishes in the Dublin diocese. For many years he worked as a scriptwriter and director making religious documentary films for Irish television and this work brought him to Europe, America, Africa and the Far East.

His first play *The True History of the Horrid Popish Plot* (1972) was an immediate success and he has followed it with several others. His most recent play is *Kolbe*, an imaginative treatment of Maximilian Kolbe's sojourn in Auschwitz, produced at the Abbey Theatre for the 1982 Dublin Theatre Festival. He has also written a number of books on historical and religious subjects.

# A SAINT IN AUSCHWITZ

## Desmond Forristal

DON BOSCO PUBLICATIONS

New Rochelle, New York

A Paperback Original
Published in Ireland as
*Maximilian of Auschwitz*
by Ward River Press, Ltd.
© 1982 Desmond Forristal

Ward River Press edition: ISBN 0-907085-38-5
Don Bosco Publications editon: ISBN 0-89944-066-5

Cover Art by Brendan Foreman
Courtesy of Brendan Foreman
and the Abbey Theater of Dublin

Made in U.S.A.

## ACKNOWLEDGEMENT

The Publishers wish to acknowledge the use of brief quotations from the following copyright publications: *I Knew Blessed Maximilian* by J. Mlodozeniec (AMI Press, Washington, N.J.); *Father Maximilian Kolbe: Fire Enkindled* by J. Burdyszek (Clonmore & Reynolds); *Commandant of Auschwitz* by Rudolf Hoess, translated by Constantine Fitzgibbon (Pan Books, Cavaye Place, London SW10 9PG; Original edition by George Weidenfeld & Nicholson); *Hitler, A Study in Tyranny* by Alan Bullock (Penguin Books). In addition, grateful acknowledgement is due to the Father General, Conventual Franciscans, Piazza SS. Apostoli, Rome, for permission to reproduce passages from Maximilian Kolbe's letters, diaries and process of beatification.

# CONTENTS

# Introduction

The little village of Oswiecim is less than two hours' journey from Cracow, the ancient capital of Poland. It is a part of Europe that has often seen war and occupation. Many of the towns and villages have two different names, one German and one Polish, reminders of the way the frontiers have shifted backwards and forwards over the centuries. Under its Polish name of Oswiecim, the village is hardly known by the outside world. Under its German name of Auschwitz, it has become one of the most infamous places in the whole sad history of man's inhumanity to man.

I visited Auschwitz on a scorching summer day in 1971. I had come to Poland to direct a series of television films on the Catholic Church in that country and one of the subjects which interested me was the story of Maximilian Kolbe. I knew little about him other than the fact that he had given his life for another man in Auschwitz. It was not until I had met some Franciscans in Cracow and heard a full account of his life and work that I realised what a remarkable man he was. The next step was to visit Auschwitz itself.

At first sight, the concentration camp seemed a pleasant, almost homely, place. A neat flower bed near the entrance, bright with summer flowers. A wrought-iron archway bearing the slogan *Arbeit*

*Macht Frei* — Work makes you Free. A broad avenue shaded by tall leafy trees. A row of friendly two-storey buildings in warm red brick, once a cavalry barracks in the days when Auschwitz was a part of the Austrian Empire. The scene was picturesque and even cosy.

Once inside any of those red-brick buildings, the atmosphere changed dramatically. The interiors had been turned into museums, each one showing a different face of the horror that was Auschwitz. There were exhibits relating to every aspect of camp life: striped prison uniforms, the pitiful daily food ration, photographs of medical experiments, tins of Cyclon B used for gassing the deportees. Maps and models traced every step of the process which brought men, women and children from every corner of occupied Europe to the gas-chamber and the crematorium.

Among all the exhibits and photographs, I was surprised at first to find no reference to Auschwitz's most famous single victim. The bookshop, filled with documentation in a dozen different languages, had nothing to offer me about Father Kolbe. However, an official readily agreed to bring me and the camera team to the cell where Kolbe had died.

As we made our way to Block 11, the Death Block, the explanation came to me. I remembered what some of my Polish contacts had told me about the official attitude to Kolbe. Even though he had not yet been beatified, the Communist authorities were worried by the cult which was growing around his name. They could not deny his heroism but they feared his hold over the hearts of the Polish people. They saw the Catholic Church as the main obstacle to the advance of Communism in Poland. They were reluctant to give any recognition or publicity to the martyrdom of a Catholic priest.

In Block 11, I was led downstairs to the basement corridor. The small cell where Kolbe and his nine companions died was as bare as it had been during the days of their agony. An iron door with a peep-hole on one side, a tiny barred window on the other, four roughly-plastered walls, a stone floor. No plaque or commemorative tablet, no official memorial of any kind. But outside the door and window there were masses of fresh-cut flowers, red and white, the national colours of Poland, brought there every morning by the hands of the faithful. The Communist rulers might wish to forget Father Kolbe and what he had done. The people of Poland remembered.

# Chapter 1
# Young Raymond

To most people outside Poland Maximilian Kolbe is known only as the priest who gave his life for another man in a concentration camp. This act is certainly his greatest claim to fame but it is not his only one. He was not some obscure figure who leaped into the limelight only with his last act. His death was of a piece with his whole life.

In Charles Dickens's novel *A Tale of Two Cities* the principal character, Sydney Carton, atones for a life of idle pleasure by going to the scaffold in place of his friend. His last words, some of the most famous in all Dickens, are: "It is a far, far better thing that I do, than I have ever done; it is a far, far better rest that I go to, than I have ever known." Maximilian Kolbe's final act of self-sacrifice was not of that kind. It was not a complete reversal of the whole previous current of his life. Rather it was the natural and logical ending of a life of exceptional selflessness and dedication, a life that would have been remarkable no matter how it ended.

Maximilian Kolbe was born on the 7th of January 1894 in the village of Zdunska Wola in the province of Lodz in Poland. The wooden house where he was born still stands and so does the parish church where he was baptised the very same day and given the name Raymond. He was the second son of Julius Kolbe and his wife Marianna, formerly Dabrowska. The name Kolbe is easier to spell and to pronounce than most Polish names and is presumably German in origin; but, as time was to show, Raymond always considered himself a Pole and nothing else.

The Kolbes, like most of their fellow-villagers, were textile weavers. Much of the space in their little home was occupied by the looms on which both parents worked in order to make a livelihood. Times were difficult and during Raymond's early years the family moved several times, ending up at Pabianice, where they settled more or less permanently.

At that period, Poland as an independent country had ceased to exist. The ancient kingdom had been carved up between its three giant neighbours, the empires of Russia, Germany and Austria. The Kolbes lived in the Russian sector, which was by far the largest of the three. The resemblance between the Poland and the Ireland of those days is striking: each an ancient nation deprived of its independence but still hoping and working and praying for its freedom. And in both countries, the Catholic Church was the great rallier and unifier of the oppressed people.

The Kolbe family were intensely Polish and intensely Catholic. As a girl Marianna Kolbe believed she had a vocation to be a nun, but she never had the opportunity of putting it to the test. The

Russian authorities suppressed convents, discouraged religious life and forbade the wearing of religious habits. As a result, it was next to impossible for a girl to follow the religious life except by going abroad. So when Julius Kolbe asked for Marianna's hand in marriage, she accepted him with a good grace, though she never ceased to believe that her true place was in the convent.

The Kolbe family finances improved a little in Pabianice. Julius continued to work as a weaver but Marianna branched out in other directions. She opened a small shop and at the same time offered her services as a midwife and general nurse to the local people. The extra money she brought in was needed to support their growing family. Five boys in all were born to Marianna Kolbe, Francis, Raymond, Joseph, Valentine and Anthony, though only the first three survived infancy.

The three boys were reared in an atmosphere of patriotism and piety. Their home, like every Polish Catholic home, had on the wall the ikon of Our Lady of Czestochowa with a light burning constantly before it. It was a national as well as a religious symbol. In 1654 a Swedish army invading Poland was defeated and driven back at the gates of the monastery of Czestochowa, where an ancient picture of the Virgin and Child had been revered for many centuries. The victory was attributed to the power of Our Lady of Czestochowa. She was given the title of Queen of Poland and copies of the miracle-working picture were venerated in every Polish household.

The religion of Julius and Marianna Kolbe could be summed up in four words: Polish, Catholic, Marian and Franciscan. The Polishness did not exclude influences from other countries, particularly France. Two apparitions to Frenchwomen had made an extraordinary impression on nineteenth-century Catholicism. The first occurred in 1830 when Catherine Labouré, a Sister of Charity in the Rue du Bac Convent in Paris, was told by the Blessed Virgin to spread devotion to her Immaculate Conception and to have a medal made in her honor. Medals and statues based on this apparition spread like wildfire through the Catholic world. So many favours were attributed to the wearing of the medal that it soon became known as the Miraculous Medal.

In 1854 Pope Pius IX formally defined the doctrine of the Immaculate Conception and declared that the Virgin Mary "in the first instant of her conception, by a singular privilege and grace granted by God in view of the merits of Jesus Christ, the Savior of the human race, was preserved exempt from all stain of original sin." Four years later, a French peasant girl named Bernadette Soubirous saw a vision of a lady in a rocky grotto who said, "I am the Immaculate Conception" and bade her uncover a spring of healing water. The place of the apparition, Lourdes, rapidly became and still remains the world's foremost center of Catholic pilgrimage.

The two aspects of devotion to the Blessed Virgin, the one traditional and the other modern, co-existed harmoniously in the Kolbe household. The ikon of Our Lady of Czestochowa was not supplanted but supplemented by the statue and medal of the Immaculate Conception. One of Raymond's early memories was of paying five kopecks to buy a statue of the Immaculate Virgin. He dated his devotion to her from that incident.

The final element in the religion of the Kolbes was devotion to St Francis, the poor man of Assisi. Both Julius and Marianna were active members of the Third Order of St Francis, the branch of the Franciscan Order which is open to married men and women. They named their first son Francis in honour of the saint. All three of their sons were later to join the Franciscans, though ironically the only one who did not stay the course was Francis himself.

In addition to his religious activities, Julius Kolbe was involved with the underground movement for Polish independence. He read patriotic literature to his sons and was at pains to instil in them an abiding awareness of the wrongs that Poland had suffered and was still suffering at the hands of her oppressors, especially Russia. Fired by his zeal, the boys played at knights and soldiers and daubed the neighbouring walls and fences with patriotic graffiti and Polish eagles, to the alarmed disapproval of their mother.

Of the two parents, Marianna seems to have been the dominant influence in the home, easily overshadowing her quieter husband. She was a firm disciplinarian and had no hesitation in using corporal punishment on her three youngsters. The boys accepted this without resentment as part of the natural order of things. Sometimes Raymond would even go and fetch the cane himself when he knew he was guilty of some misdemeanour.

One of his childish scrapes gave rise to the best-known incident of his childhood. The source of the story is his mother, who told it only after his death. Apparently she rebuked him one day when he was about ten and said to him, "Raymond, whatever will become of you?" Soon afterwards she noticed a marked improvement in his behaviour. He seemed to have become more serious, more obedient, more devout. He spent a good deal of his time praying in front of the shrine of Our Lady in the home. She asked him what had caused the change and eventually and with some difficulty wormed the story out of him. This is what he told her:

> When you scolded me, Mother, I prayed a lot to Our Lady and I asked her to tell me what would become of me. Afterwards when I was in the Church, I prayed again, and then Our Lady appeared to me holding two crowns in her hand, one white and the other red. She looked at me kindly and she asked me if I wanted these two crowns. The white one meant that I would always remain pure and the red one meant that I would be a martyr. I said I wanted them. Then she gave me a loving look and disappeared.

The incident, if it happened, was a prophetic one. Many of the pictures of Kolbe that circulate in Poland today show Our Lady in the background holding the two crowns, an apt summary of everything he lived and died for. But one would feel happier about the authenticity of the story if it had come from himself or, failing that, if it had been told while he was still alive to confirm or deny it.

Life in the Kolbe home was hard but not unhappy. Both parents were thrifty and hard-working and gradually their economic situation improved. The Polish winter was long and severe but no doubt the boys enjoyed playing in the snow and sliding or skating on the frozen ponds; and there was always a warm stove and a bowl of hot beetroot soup to come home to. Then came the glorious Polish summer, week after week of shimmering heat, culminating in the annual pilgrimage to Czestochowa for the 15th of August, the Feast of the Assumption of the Virgin Mary.

The Kolbe family regularly made the pilgrimage, joining the huge crowds who walked hundreds of miles from all over Poland to the hill on which the monastery was built, Jasna Gora, the Mountain of Light. They marched across the endless Polish plains, past fields of waving wheat and tall nodding sunflowers, singing hymns and counting their beads, waiting for the joyful moment when the tip of the monastery's spire appeared over the horizon.

They poured into the little town of Czestochowa, ablaze with banners and flags and the brightly coloured costumes of the different provinces. They made their way up the hill, past the rows of shops and booths with their gaudy statues and pictures and rosary beads, through the great arched gateway of the monastery, into the baroque splendours of the church. Finally, by dint of patience and pushing, they found themselves in the side chapel where the sacred image was to be seen, encrusted with silver and jewels and surrounded by hundreds of candles and votive lamps. Here in this tiny crowded spot, where the silence was broken only by the murmurs of prayers and the slow shuffling of the passing pilgrims, beat the true heart of Poland.

The gradual improvement in the family finances made it possible for the parents to start thinking about their boys' education. There was no free education in Russian Poland but Pabianice had a small commercial school which undertook to equip boys for a business career on payment of a modest fee. At first the family could afford only to send Francis, the eldest. Raymond stayed at home and looked after the shop during his mother's frequent absences in the course of her duties as nurse and midwife. He also cooked the family meals on these occasions and is said to have developed quite a skill in cookery.

At the same time, his own education was not completely neglected. In addition to what he learned from his parents at home, Raymond was given some lessons by the parish priest, Father Jakuski, and by a kindly local chemist, Mr Kotowski, who was impressed by the lad's intelligence when he called to the shop to collect medicine for one of his mother's patients. He proved an apt and willing pupil and when the Kolbes at length could afford to send him to the commercial school he was able to join the same class as his elder brother.

In 1907, when Raymond was thirteen, a retreat was preached in Pabianice by Father Peregrine Haczela, Provincial of the Conventual Franciscans. It was to be a turning point in the life of Raymond and indeed of the whole Kolbe family. The Conventual Franciscans are a branch of the Order of St Francis who are strong in Central Europe and the United States of America. They are called Conventual because of their custom of living in large convents or monasteries, unlike other Franciscans who tend to form smaller communities. They also differ from other Franciscans in wearing black habits rather than brown ones, and it is from this that they get their popular nickname of Black Franciscans.

In 1907 their Polish headquarters was in Galicia, the Austrian sector of Poland, in the town which was known to the Poles as Lwow and to the Austrians as Lemberg. (Connoisseurs of Polish toponymy may like to know that the Germans called it Löwenburg, the Italians called it Leopoli, and the Ruthenians called it Lwihohrod). Austria was the only one of the three occupying powers which was sympathetic to the Catholic Church and it was in Galicia that Polish Catholic institutions had most freedom of organisation. The Conventual Franciscans had a novitiate there for the education of future priests and also a preparatory school or minor seminary for young boys who hoped one day to enter the novitiate.

The Kolbes attended the retreat given by Father Haczela, children as well as parents. The devotion of the family to St Francis combined with the eloquence of the preacher made an impression on all of them, but particularly on the two eldest sons. The retreat crystallised thoughts that had been forming in their minds for months and even years. They decided that God was calling them to be Franciscans and they applied to Father Haczela for admission to the minor seminary. The priest was impressed by them, the parents raised no objection, and arrangements were made for them to begin their schooling at Lwow later that same year.

The journey to Lwow was something of an adventure. Not only were the two boys leaving parents and home for the first time, they were breaking the law by going out of Russian territory without official authorization. But the frontier was long and loosely guarded and, with their father guiding them, they reached the city of Cracow in Austrian territory without mishap. There they parted, Julius returning to Pabianice, Francis and Raymond continuing on by train to Lwow.

# Chapter 2
# The Black Franciscan

After the narrow provincialism of Pabianice, Lwow must have seemed to pulse with cultural, intellectual and religious activity. The 1910 edition of *The Catholic Encyclopaedia* gives a contemporary description of the city as it presented itself to the eyes of the two young Kolbes.

> Lemberg is situated in a deep and narrow valley on the Pelter, a tributary of the Bug. The capital of the Austrian Kingdom of Galicia and Lodomeria, it contains — including its many and populous suburbs — about 160,000 inhabitants, of whom 45,000 are Jews. Of the convents which, in the seventeenth century, gained for it the name of the "City of Monks", some still exist . . . The national Ossolinski Institute possesses a library of the highest value for the study of Polish literature and local history, containing more than 100,000 volumes and 4000 manuscripts. The University, founded in 1660 by Casimir of Poland, now numbers about 200 professors and tutors, with 1900 students, 300 of whom attend the faculty of Catholic theology. The city also possesses a large number of educational estab-

lishments for boys and girls, besides many benevolent institutions.

The next three years passed happily and uneventfully for the two brothers. Raymond, the younger, soon proved the more impressive personality. He showed the first signs of those qualities which were to mark his later career: leadership, decisiveness, the ability to plan broadly and imaginatively while at the same time taking care of even the smallest details. He excelled in the practical sciences, gaining his highest marks in mathematics and physics. He showed his interest in military affairs by drawing up in his free time elaborate plans for fortifying Lwow against a possible Russian attack. The air was full of rumors of war and revolution and it was beginning to look as if the time was coming when Poland could once again rise against her oppressors, this time successfully.

After their three years in the minor seminary, the time came for the two boys to make formal applications to enter the novitiate. As the decisive day drew nearer, Raymond found that his former certainty was deserting him. He still wished to serve God and his Immaculate Mother but he was less and less sure of how this was to be done. Should it be as a priest of the Order of St Francis or should it be as a soldier in the Polish army of liberation for which recruits were already being sought? "I bowed down before her altar," he wrote later, "and promised the Most Holy Virgin that I would fight for her. But how? I didn't know, but it seemed to me that it must be by force of arms."

The day of decision arrived and Raymond had still not made up his mind. Frantic last-minute consultations with Francis were of no avail, as the elder brother was quite happy to let the younger make the decision for both of them. Finally Raymond decided that their first duty was to fight for the freedom of their country and the docile Francis accepted without demur.

The unexpected arrival of his mother prevented Raymond from carrying out his resolve. Writing to her nine years later, he recalled the events of that fateful day.

> I was on my way to Father Provincial to tell him that Francis and I didn't wish to enter the Order when I heard the sound of the bell summoning me to the parlor. The good God in his infinite mercy, through the intercession of the Immaculate, had sent you, Mother, to visit me at this most critical moment.

Some time earlier Maximilian's mother and father had made an unusual decision. Their third son, Joseph, had expressed his resolve to join his two brothers as a Franciscan. With all their sons now dedicating themselves to God, the parents decided to do the same. Julius went to a Franciscan monastery in Cracow and Marianna to a Benedictine Convent in Lwow. Her girlhood dream of becoming a nun was at last to be realised; and now she was able to offer to God not just herself but her husband and her three sons as well.

What passed between mother and son in the parlor on that day we are not told. It is safe to say that she is hardly likely to have shown much pleasure at the news that her two eldest sons were about to abandon the religious life. The result was that Raymond rapidly re-thought his position, Francis once again followed obediently, and they asked the Father Provincial to admit them to the novitiate. However strangely arrived at, the decision was one which Raymond was never to regret.

On the 4th of September 1910 the two youths began their novitiate in Lwow. It was the custom at that time to take a new name on entering a religious order to symbolise the beginning of a new life. Raymond became Brother Maximilian, Francis became Brother Valerian. No reason for the choice of these names is known. It is quite possible that they were simply assigned these names by their superiors, without any choice in the matter. Along with their new names, the novices were given the habit of the Order, the black robe with its cape and hood, the girdle and large rosary beads.

The year of novitiate is a time of probation for both the novice and the Order. The two have the opportunity to come to know one another and to decide whether they want to make the relationship permanent. Under the guidance of a novice-master, the novice is instructed in the practice of prayer and the Christian virtues, in the nature of the religious life and in the rule and traditions of his Order. At the end of the year, with the consent of both sides, the ceremony of simple profession commits the novice to the Order and the Order to him. The commitment is not permanent until the solemn profession is made some years later.

Brother Maximilian made his simple profession on the 5th of September 1911. He was seventeen years of age. He was kept on in Lwow for a further year to complete his general education before beginning the study of philosophy and theology. He was then transferred to Cracow but was destined to stay there only briefly. His superiors decided that in view of his academic abilities he should be sent to study in Rome. From Cracow he wrote to his mother in Lwow to tell her the news. It is the earliest letter of his that survives and for that reason it is worth giving in full.

Cracow, 28 X 1912

Praised be Jesus Christ!

Dearest Mother,

When you were here with us, we told you that five clerics from Lwow and two from Cracow were to go abroad for their studies. Now the Father Provincial has directed that seven clerics are to go, but all of them from our house in Lwow, because those from Cracow would find it too difficult on account of the different arrangement of the program of theological studies in the different places.

One of us — Maximilian — is to go to Rome for philosophy, and to attend the Gregorian University.

My other companions have gone for a few days to their families but I have stayed on because Father lives here and I saw you at the end of the holidays; hardly any of the others have been home for three years. In compensation, for the last two days I have been allowed to spend as much time as I want with Father.

I haven't written to Joseph, because I am sure that you, Mother, will go to see him on the Feast of All Saints and tell him all the news.

Finally I ask you to say a special prayer for me. That is all I need. As regards everything else, the Holy Religious Order will be the best of mothers to me. The dangers over there are very great. I have heard, for instance, that even the religious are accosted by low women, and in spite of this I will be required to walk to the college and back every day.

I would also be glad, Mother, if you would ask Joseph to remember me at Holy Communion and to say a prayer to St Anthony for me, no matter how short. If that saint, as Joseph once told me in a letter, never refused him anything, then he will surely listen to him now and protect me.

I am all ready for the journey. We leave this evening and we will arrive at our destination about midday on Wednesday if we get an express train. At 13 hours we will probably be at Pontebbe and at 22 hours at Bologna (the Italians count the hours up to 24).

After the journey I am sure I will have interesting things to write about.

We ask your prayers with all our hearts.

Your ever grateful sons,

Maximilian.

The use of the plural at the beginning and end suggests that Francis (Valerian) was supposed to sign the letter as well, but he failed to do so. He stayed on in Cracow for his studies while Maximilian left that same evening as scheduled. He was not to see his mother or his brothers again for seven years. He was never to see his father again.

Two days and nights of travelling brought Maximilian and his six companions safely to Rome. They stayed in the Seraphic College in the Via di San Teodoro and walked each day to their lectures in the Gregorian University. Maximilian discovered that the reports about the wild women of Rome had been somewhat exaggerated. He wrote to his mother:

The situation here is not as bad as I told you in my earlier letter. The Italians have other things to do besides bothering us. Anyhow, we usually go in a group; so anyone who wants to molest us had better think whether he mightn't get back as good as he gives.

In the Gregorian University, Maximilian attended lectures on philosophy and mathematics. He had no difficulty with the prescribed subjects and his active questing mind led him down all kinds of unexpected side roads as well. His interest in science and technology remained as lively as ever. He became fascinated with the idea of space travel and he invented a vehicle which he was convinced could be used for reaching the moon and planets. He called it the ethereoplane and some of his drawings and technical descriptions of it still survive.

At the same time he was visiting the sights of Rome and his letters home contain many descriptions of the churches and monuments of the city. He describes the Colosseum, the Catacombs, the ruins of Caesar's palace. He attends a ceremony in St Peter's where a Cardinal blesses the congregation with the veil of St Veronica: with the aid of a confrère's binoculars, he manages to make out the impression of Christ's face on the veil. He gets a ticket which allows him to go into the Vatican and attend an audience of Pope Benedict XIV in the courtyard of St Damasus.

We do not have Marianna Kolbe's letters to her son but it is not hard to reconstruct their contents from his replies. Her vocation to the religious life had not worked out as smoothly as she had hoped. She was still living with the Benedictine nuns in Lwow but not as a member of the community. No convent seemed anxious to accept as a postulant a rather emotional middle-aged woman with a husband somewhere in the background. Maximilian made various inquiries through his contacts without success. In one letter he tells her that a priest friend of his has tried three convents on her behalf.

> The first one said they didn't accept anyone over a certain age. The second, a Bavarian one, said they didn't accept anyone who didn't come from Bavaria. The third one said they didn't accept anyone at all, because they didn't even have enough food for themselves.

Eventually in 1913 Marianna took up residence with the Felician Sisters in Cracow. She never became a nun herself but she seems to have found the spiritual home she sought with the Felicians, since she remained there until her death in 1946.

Her husband, Julius, was also having problems with his vocation. It is hard to avoid the feeling that it was not his vocation at all but his wife's, and that she had talked him into the idea as part of her grand plan for the future of the Kolbe family. In any event, Julius did not stay with the Franciscans in Cracow. The correspondence between him and Maximilian has been lost and it is impossible to trace his movements over the next few years. One account says that he went to Czestochowa and made a living there by selling religious objects to the pilgrims.

In the early part of 1914 a curious incident occurred to Maximilian. He describes it in a letter to his mother written on the 4th of April.

Nothing unusual has happened here except this: I very nearly lost a finger from my right hand. I developed something in the nature of an abscess. In spite of the treatment given by the college doctor, the pus refused to dry up. After some time, the doctor noticed that the bone itself was beginning to be affected. It would be necessary to have a small surgical operation in order to scrape the bone. When I heard this, I said that I had in my possession a better medicine. Actually I had been given a little Lourdes water by Father Rector. When he gave it to me, he told me the story of his own remarkable cure.

At the age of twelve, he was suffering from a diseased foot. A bone in the sole of the foot was gradually turning gangrenous and he couldn't sleep with the pain. At times it made him scream aloud. The foot would have to be amputated. One day the doctors were to meet for a consultation. His mother, realising the situation, tried a completely new treatment as a last resort. She pulled the bandages off the foot, washed it with soap, and then rinsed it with miraculous water from Lourdes. For the first time Father Rector fell asleep. After fifteen minutes he woke up. He was cured.

It was clearly a miracle; but the doctor, who was an unbeliever, insisted on explaining it some other way. But then a few days later, a piece of diseased bone came away from the foot and the doctor found himself with an extraordinary fact: the bone was gone completely gangrenous but it had detached itself and come out in a miraculous way. As a result of this, the doctor was converted and undertook to build a church at his own expense. Father Rector, after the miraculous water was applied, had been fully cured and was able to walk, but he had been unable to put on his shoe on account of the protrusion which still remained. When the diseased bone came away, everything went back to normal again.

Anyhow, when our doctor heard that I had some Lourdes water, he was happy to bathe me with it himself. And what happened? The next day, instead of having the operation on the bone, I heard from the surgeon in the hospital that an operation was no longer needed. After some dressings had been put on it, I was completely cured. Glory to God and to the Immaculate!

The healing of the finger would hardly be accounted a miracle if measured by the stringent standards of the Medical Bureau in Lourdes. Still, it is understandable that the young Maximilian, faced with the possible loss of a finger, should have regarded the cure as a singular favor and that it further strengthened his devotion to the Immaculate Virgin — or "The Immaculate," as he had now begun to call her. The use of the feminine adjective Immaculate *(Niepokalana)* without any noun was as unusual in Polish then as it is in English now, and this was the first time it occurred in Maximilian's writings. From this time on it became his usual way of referring to the Mother of God and within a few years, due to his influence, it was to become familiar throughout Poland.

# Chapter 3
# Father Maximilian

On the 28th of June 1914 the Archduke Ferdinand, heir to the Austrian throne, was assassinated in Sarajevo. It was the spark which set off the Great War. Within a few weeks the five great powers of Europe were involved, with Germany and Austria on the one side ranged against Britain, France and Russia on the other. Italy remained neutral for the moment.

The Poles saw in the Great War the chance for them to regain their independence. The Austrian government now encouraged the underground Polish army to emerge into the open and to fight against the Russians who controlled by far the largest part of Poland. Julius Kolbe was quick to enlist. He was made an officer and assigned to a detachment operating in the Olkusz region. His eldest son, Brother Valerian, also heard once again the call to arms and this time decided to answer it. He left his monastery in Cracow and joined the Polish army as plain Francis Kolbe.

Maximilian watched all these developments with understandable forebodings which were heightened by an almost complete breakdown of communications between Rome and Cracow. A Christmas card which he sent to his mother on the 24th of

December 1914 did however manage to reach its destination.

> I didn't write earlier because we had classes up to yesterday; and now I'm only sending you a card because it has a better chance of reaching you. Since your last letter, which came before the holidays, I have heard nothing from you, Mother, maybe because a lot of correspondence is getting lost, especially letters. It's a year now since I had any post from Father. How is he? And how is Joseph? What is Brother Valerian's address?
>
> This year it's hard to wish anyone "Happy Christmas." at least we can wish that the Infant Jesus will bring peace to our poor country and to the whole of Europe.

When Maximilian was writing this card, his father was probably dead. In September his company had been surrounded by the Russians and taken prisoner. About what happened next only one thing is certain: Julius Kolbe was never seen or heard of again. According to the most likely account, he was executed by the Russians, possibly because as a former inhabitant of the Russian sector he was regarded as a traitor. He died as he had lived, a slightly shadowy, slightly out-of-focus figure, tinged with an air of gentle failure. Yet he was a good man and a brave man and he passed on these qualities in full measure to his sons. In them, if nowhere else, he had his just memorial.

Meanwhile, unaware of his father's fate, Maximilian continued with the normal life of a Franciscan student. In October 1914 he made his solemn profession, committing himself permanently to the Order of Conventual Franciscans. He took the additional name of Mary and from now on signed himself Maximilian M. Kolbe in formal correspondence. He had completed the normal two years of philosophical studies but he had shown so much talent that he was directed to study for his doctorate.

A crisis threatened in May 1915 when Italy entered the war against Austria. Some of the Poles had to leave Italy because of their Austrian citizenship. Maximilian was sent by his superiors to the little independent state of San Marino while the complicated question of his nationality was sorted out. Eventually the Italian authorities agreed that he was a native of Russia and therefore an ally, and he was allowed back to Rome after an absence of about four weeks. He took this interruption to his studies in his stride and he was awarded the degree of Doctor of Philosophy in October at the age of only twenty-one. Two weeks later he began his study of theology in the Franciscan International College in Rome.

The war did not greatly affect the life of the Roman colleges and universities. The students followed the usual round of studies, examinations and spiritual exercises, with a couple of months' break each summer when they went to their summer house or *villa* in the hills to escape the heat and the mosquitoes. Like his fellow students, Maximilian was pious, industrious and a little naive. His intelligence and application were above average but he did not attract undue attention to himself. It was only many years later, after his death, that his Roman contemporaries began to recall little things he had done and said that had lodged in their memories.

In those years before the signing of the Lateran Treaty, Rome was a bitterly divided city. The Pope still claimed civil jurisdiction over the city and the former Papal States which had been forcibly wrested from him by the Italian government. The supporters and opponents of the Papal claims often clashed in the streets, physically as well as verbally.

As his familiarity with the city and his command of the Italian language grew, Maximilian was quite ready to face any opponent and to give as good as he got, at least on the level of words. On one occasion he was overheard in vigorous debate with a freethinker who tried to clinch the argument by declaring that he was a doctor of philosophy; the wind was taken out of his sails when the youthful student, preferring truth to modesty, declared that he was a doctor of philosophy too. Another time, Maximilian challenged a gang of loutish youths who were insulting a wayside shrine to the Madonna and rebuked them for their conduct. Some hint of authority in his voice silenced them and they dispersed in a somewhat shame-faced manner.

At that time most of the anti-clericalism was

attributed to the Freemasons, not without cause. The Italian Freemasons, unlike their Anglo-Saxon counterparts, were committed to the destruction of the influence of the Catholic Church and were fond of organising anti-religious processions and demonstrations. Maximilian decided that the simplest way of solving the problem was by converting the leader of the Freemasons and he asked permission for himself and a companion to visit the Grand Master in his headquarters and convince him of the error of his ways. In planning this, he was only following the precedent set by St Francis himself who once went to Egypt to convert the Sultan and succeeded in having a courteous exchange of views with that monarch though not in converting him. But Maximilian's superior was unimpressed by the historical parallel and ordered the young man to confine himself to praying for the Grand Master's soul.

Innocent of the world in some ways, Maximilian was surprisingly sophisticated in others. This was particularly noticeable in his attitude to the communications media. Many of the students followed the lead of the older clergy in taking a negative attitude to the media, denouncing the press as anti-clerical, the cinema as pornographic, and so on. Maximilian took the opposite view. He held very strongly that such media as the press and the cinema could be just as effective for good as for evil. He advocated the setting up of religious newspapers and magazines and he even started to work on a scheme for introducing sound to the cinema and producing talking films, something which no one had yet succeeded in doing.

These were minor incidents. Two major events occurred during these years when Maximilian prepared for his ordination to the priesthood. One was his founding of the Militia of the Immaculate. The other was his discovery that he was suffering from tuberculosis of the lungs.

Older readers will have no difficulty in remembering the dread which the word tuberculosis used to inspire, particularly among the young. The tubercular youth or maiden was a mainstay of romantic fiction and they coughed their way through innumerable novels, plays and operas. In real life the disease was equally dangerous and a good deal less romantic. The disease typically made itself known in the late teens and early twenties and young people in that age group learned to fear any cough, especially if it persisted beyond a week or two. The coughing of blood was the clinching sign that the lungs had been affected. Methods of prevention were unknown, the treatment was long and uncertain, and even when the patient was declared cured there was always the danger of a relapse. The first spot of blood on the handkerchief came with the sickening force of a death sentence.

Maximilian has left us an account of how he became aware of the disease. One day during the summer of 1917 he and some of his companions were at the summer house of their Order and they began to play a game of football. Suddenly, in the middle of the game, he felt a warm flow coming up his throat. It was blood. He lay down on the grass for a while but the blood kept coming. At length it stopped and he was hurried to a doctor who sent him back to the College in a coach and ordered him to stay in bed.

The haemorrhaging and the pain continued for some days. After about two weeks it had ceased and he recovered a little strength. The doctor allowed him to go back to the *villa* in the company of another cleric. He was greeted joyfully by the other students and he recalls how they brought him fresh figs and bread to eat and wine to drink. He was still weak but his mind had all the clarity and urgency of the consumptive. He took the opportunity that same day to reveal to two of the students the plan he had been meditating for some months. Their reaction was favourable.

When he was strong enough to travel, he was sent to convalesce in Viterbo in company with another student, who was also drawn into the plan Then Maximilian returned to Rome and resumed his studies as if nothing had happened.

It seems extraordinary that so little attention was paid to his condition. The exact dates are un-certain but there can hardly have been more than two or three months between the first haemorrhage and his resumption of normal student life. It is hardly possible that the doctors could have misread symptoms which were so tragically common at that time. The normal course of treatment would have involved confinement to bed in a sanatorium for a period of at least six months and generally much longer. It is likely indeed that Maximilian made light of his condition, anxious as he was to get his plan under way while he still had some health and strength left: but one cannot acquit the doctors of the charge of having made a near-fatal error in his case.

The plan which Maximilian had been revolving in his mind since the beginning of the year was nothing less than this: the conversion of the world through the intercession of the Immaculate. The idea had come to him one morning while he was at prayer and having thought it over he went to consult his confessor and spiritual director. The confessor may have smiled inwardly at this simplistic and naive master-plan but he did nothing to discourage the young man. He may have discerned in him not just the generosity and enthusiasm of youth, but also some fore-shadowing of that tenacity and fixity of purpose which were to become so marked in his later life. In time to come the young man would find out how grand general schemes can come to grief on the practical problems of daily life: but he would have the natural and super-natural resources to deal with those problems and triumphantly overcome them.

Having sounded out various companions during the summer months, the months of his illness, Maximilian decided the time had come to launch his crusade. The first meeting took place on the evening of the 16th of October 1917 in the Franciscan International College. Seven young men were present, all of them students of the College and members of the Order of Conventual Franciscans. There were three Italians, three Rumanians and one Pole, Maximilian himself.

Fearing discouragement and even ridicule from older brethren, the seven met secretly in one of their rooms. They set up in their midst a little altar to the Immaculate, a statue between two lighted candles. Maximilian produced a small piece of paper on which he had written down the aims of the organisation and read it to them. They approved it and added their signatures. Next they went to the chapel where one of them who was a priest blessed miraculous medals and imposed them on each of those present. Then they went back to their rooms.

It had not been a very exciting meeting. At least one of the seven decided that the whole thing was a product of youthful folly and tried to persuade the others of this as well. No new members were added and the existing members confined themselves to praying and to distributing miraculous medals. The only one who showed any enthusiasm was Maximilian. The first step had been taken. The venture was under the protection of the Immaculate. He had no doubt about the outcome.

On the 28th of April 1918 Maximilian was ordained priest by Cardinal Pompili in the Church of S. Andrea della Valle in Rome. The war was still raging in Europe and none of his family were present at the ceremony. He wrote his mother a long description of the occasion which ended with these ominous words: "As for me, I will have a lot of things to tell you; God willing, I will tell you face to face, if I am still alive." The last phrase looks like a cryptic reference to his ill health, the only reference found in any of his letters at this time. He was never one to parade his woes or cause useless worry to others.

The latter part of 1918 did in fact see a recurrence of the haemorrhages. A new and unexpected danger threatened him in October when the so-called Spanish flu struck Rome. This was a particularly virulent form of influenza which swept through the world in the closing months of 1918. Its effect on a Europe already ravaged by four years of war and hunger was devastating for young and old alike. An estimated twenty million people died in the epidemic, most of them of pneumonia resulting from infection of the lungs.

Maximilian survived the epidemic, though his tubercular lungs must have given him anxious moments. Some of his companions were not so fortunate. Among them were two of the original seven members of the Militia, who died within a few days of each other towards the end of October. Though naturally grief-stricken, Maximilian saw the hand of God in their deaths. He believed that they had been called home by the Immaculate to complete in Heaven the work they had begun on earth and to help the fledgling organisation with their prayers.

It was in fact from this moment that the Militia began to expand. The survivors were filled with a new enthusiasm and began to recruit increasing numbers of members for their association. Maximilian himself wrote to his brother Joseph, now Brother Alphonsus in the Franciscan house in Cracow, enclosing a copy of the Constitution of the Militia of the Immaculate and asking him to become a member himself and recruit others in Poland for the M.I. The Constitution of the M.I. read as follows:

## MILITIA OF THE IMMACULATE

"She shall crush the head of the serpent."
(Gen. 3: 15)
"You alone have conquered all the heresies in the world."               (Office of Our Lady)

### I   Purpose
To bring about the conversion of sinners, heretics, schismatics, etc., and particularly Freemasons, and the sanctification of all mankind through the patronage and mediation of the B.V.M. Immaculate.

### II   Conditions
1. The total offering of oneself to the B.V.M. Immaculate as an instrument in her hands.
2. The wearing of the Miraculous Medal.

### III   Means
1. To pray every day to the Immaculate using the aspiration: "O Mary conceived without sin, pray for us who have recourse to you and

for all who do not have recourse to you,
especially Freemasons."
2. To use all lawful means according to the
opportunities offered by one's state and condition of life, as each one's zeal and prudence
may suggest; and especially to spread the
Miraculous Medal.

Brother Alphonsus was, as he later confessed,
somewhat baffled by this document. He prudently
decided to put it aside and take no further action
until such time as his brother should have returned
to Poland and explained his plans in greater detail.

That return was not far off. But first there was
one more laurel to be gathered. Maximilian's
ordination did not signify the end of his studies.
His superiors decided that he should complete his
study of theology by acquiring the degree of Doctor
of Divinity. Obedient and industrious as ever,
Maximilian went back to his books and his lectures.

His last letter from Rome to his mother was
written on the 20th of April, 1919. He makes no
mention of his own troubles but he is full of
concern for his family in Poland. Francis had survived the war and was now asking to be re-admitted
to the Franciscans, but they were unwilling to take
him back.

It was Francis whose example brought me to
this haven of salvation; I wanted to leave and
to dissuade him as well from entering the novitiate. But now . . . Every day, in the "memen-

to" of the Mass I offer him to the Immaculate and I trust (as you do too, Mother) that sooner or later she will obtain pity for him from the mercy of God.

As for Father, I don't know what to say. Every day I remember him at Holy Mass. If I had any definite news of his death, I could at least say Mass for his soul and we could have a sung Mass for him in the college, as is the custom. But what if he is still alive? Father Rector has given me permission to make whatever inquiries I can by means of the Russian newspapers. I know a Russian citizen here so I will see if anything can be arranged. I have put the whole problem into the hands of the Immaculate, our Mother, and she can solve it as she pleases.

Do you remember, Mother, the time I had to do the examination for the commercial school? You said that if I passed it, you would become a queen; and Father said he would become a bishop. With the help of God through the intercession of the Immaculate, I did pass it. You, Mother, could say that you got your wish, but Father? I leave everything to the mercy of God, to the Immaculate.

As for Brother Alphonsus, praised be God through the Immaculate for all he has done for him. He has been greatly blessed. But you must pray that he will persevere to the end and that he will ever grow in love without limits. Dear Mother, pray for the same thing for me, especially for that "without limits," so that I too can ever grow in that love as quickly as possible.

On the 22nd of July 1919, at the age of twenty-five, Maximilian was awarded the degree of Doctor of Divinity. He now had two doctorates, one in philosophy and one in theology. The following day he left Rome for Poland.

# Chapter 4
# Return to Poland

The Poland to which the young Father Kolbe returned in 1919 was very different from the one he had left eight years earlier. First and foremost, it was now a free and independent nation once again. The three mighty empires which had oppressed it had all been humbled by military defeat and internal revolt. The Bolshevik revolution of 1917 had taken Russia out of the war and the military reverses of 1918 had forced Austria and Germany to sue for peace. The Poles dated their independence from Armistice Day, the 11th of November 1918.

Independence still left Poland with many problems. The country had been devastated by four years of constant battles across its territory. Millions of its people had died as a result of military action or the famine and disease that followed. Agriculture had been disrupted, industry shattered, towns and villages ravaged. The economy was in ruins and galloping inflation had brought about a collapse of the currency. To add to all their worries, the Bolsheviks were reasserting Russian claims to Polish territory and were preparing an invasion from the east. But in spite of everything, there was a spirit of hope and determination in the country that was destined to overcome all these obstacles.

The young priest who alighted from the train in Cracow on the 29th of July was almost a microcosm of the new Poland: physically a wreck, but armed with a faith and a courage that transcended all physical limitations. The re-union with his mother and brothers must have been an occasion of great joy, but of joy tinged with apprehension. The inroads that the disease had made on the young man could not be concealed from the eyes of those that loved him.

His first appointment as a priest was a teaching one. He was assigned to the Major Seminary of the Franciscans in Cracow with the duty of teaching Church history to the students. It was not a very demanding duty and was for that reason suited to his delicate state of health. But instead of resting in his free time, Maximilian pushed ahead tirelessly with the founding and spreading of the Militia in Poland.

It was not to prove a particularly happy time for him. With the students he soon established good relations and many of them enrolled at once in the Militia, undertaking to wear the Miraculous Medal and recite the daily prayer. But his relations with his fellow priests were uneasy and led to a good deal of suffering for Maximilian.

It was partly his own fault. It was understandable that some of the older priests should resent this young man, barely out of the seminary, telling his seniors what they ought to do to convert the world. He was pushing his new organisation as a panacea for all ills to people who knew from long and hard experience that there is no such thing as a panacea for all ills.

In addition, his personal manner was unattractive. Much of this was due to his illness, but since he rarely complained others did not always realize this. Because of the danger of haemorrhages, he moved slowly and cautiously. Because of his damaged lungs, his voice was low and sometimes difficult to hear. An older priest who found himself buttonholed by this intense and slightly creepy young man and subjected to a long and only partially audible harangue on the necessity of joining his organization might be forgiven for feeling a little impatient.

These misunderstandings were a great grief to Maximilian. It is those who are closest to us that have the greatest power to wound us. We can steel ourselves readily enough against those who call themselves our enemies. But to be hurt by those who are our friends and brothers, that is to be hurt indeed.

Some of this hurt comes out in a talk he gave on the 18th of September to the seminarians who had joined the M.I. Ostensibly he was speaking about what happened in Rome but his words could also apply to his experiences in Poland, both then and later.

> I am speaking of the persecution which can come to us from reasonable people, including some enrolled in the ranks of the M.I., all of it

with the best of intentions in those who oppose us. Truly, it is most painful, if one does not put all one's trust in God through the Immaculate, to see someone full of zeal for the greater glory of God crossing us at every turn and trying to destroy or ruin what has been built up. Perhaps having once been deeply involved in the work of the M.I. such a person will afterwards draw away and begin suggesting doubts to others, sowing distrust and indifference.

Nor is this all, for we ourselves are changeable. What we accept today with enthusiasm will tomorrow seem tiresome. What today attracts us will tomorrow frighten us because of the number and heaviness of the sacrifices it demands. And in this case we note that the difficulty rises from self love.

Faced with all this, where shall we find relief? What shall we lean on for support in all these difficulties? Our support must be something very steady and unchangeable, something that can serve as an immovable foundation, in a word, something of God: and this can only be a holy and unswerving obedience to the Immaculate, who reveals her will through our superiors.

Maximilian was never one to give in to difficulties and discouragement. Gradually the enrolment book of the M.I. began to fill up. Thirty-three sisters from the Poor Clare Convent in Cracow joined up, followed by ten cadets from the army training school in Przemysl. In his letters, Maximilian notes the latest membership statistics: in one letter he gives 966 at the beginning but is able to raise it to 985 by the time he gets to the postscript. The momentum increased rapidly and the hundreds became thousands. The M.I. seemed to be touching some deep nerve in the Catholic Poland of 1920.

The parallels with the Ireland of that time are striking. Ireland too was emerging violently into independence after centuries of oppression. In each case the winning of political freedom was accompanied by a revival of traditional religious devotion, notably devotion to the Blessed Virgin. The very forms that the devotion took were similar. The Militia of the Immaculate in Poland had a close counterpart in the Legion of Mary in Ireland.

The first meeting of the Legion of Mary took place in Dublin in 1921 as the struggle for independence neared its end. A group of young people gathered in a room around a statue of the Immaculate Virgin flanked by two lighted candles. They prayed together and discussed how best to serve God under the patronage of his Blessed Mother. It was almost a carbon copy of the first meeting of the M.I. The similarity extends even to the military titles chosen by both organisations.

The Legion of Mary had some advantages over the M.I. which help to account for its more rapid spread throughout the world. From the start it was oriented towards action as well as prayer and it laid down a minimum requirement of attending a me-

ing and doing some apostolic work every week.
The commitment demanded by the M.I. was much
smaller — the saying of a short daily prayer and the
wearing of a medal — and as a result, while members joined easily, they also left easily and almost
unnoticeably. This was something which was to
cause concern to Maximilian, though not until
some time later.

At this time he had something much more
urgent to worry about. In the summer of 1920 he
was sent to Lwow to do temporary duty for a
priest who was dying of tuberculosis. He himself
was almost as ill as the man he was replacing. He
had another relapse and the local doctor examined
him. This good man, Dr Rencki by name, did what
should have been done a long time ago: he insisted
that his patient should go to a sanatorium and stay
there until he was cured. The doctor had his way
and on the 11th of August Maximilian arrived at
the sanatorium in Zakopane for what was to be a
long stay.

Zakopane was a pleasant little resort town lying
high in the Tatra Mountains in the extreme south
of Poland. The clean air and bracing climate made
it a favourite place for sufferers from tuberculosis.
The drugs which are now used to counter the
disease had not yet been discovered and the
principal treatment was simply to send the patient
to a sanatorium until he either got better or died.
The patient often did recover. Rest, fresh air, good
food, and the absence of tension and stress helped

the body to mobilise its natural resources and overcome the alien bacillus. In extreme cases, lung
surgery was also resorted to.

Maximilian had no sooner arrived than he sent
off a postcard to his mother. The tone was cheerful
without being particularly optimistic.

> Dear Mother,
> Here I am at my destination. Even if I can't
> walk in the mountains like the priest in the
> picture on the card, I am in the right place for
> a cure. Here I can really follow the doctor's
> orders. The air is great, there is even a veranda
> where you can sit outdoors on a deckchair,
> the food is very good and you can have what-
> ever you want. God's will be done, whether
> the disease is to persist or to get worse or to
> get better or to disappear entirely.
> Your ever loving son,
> Fr Maximilian M.

He was to stay in Zakopane for eight months, followed by a further six months' convalescence in
Nieszawa. Fourteen months of inactivity was a
heavy burden for him to bear: but it saved his life.
The term "inactivity" is in any event a relative one.
Maximilian's inactivity did not mean that he ceased
to take a keen interest in the progress of the M.I.
or to keep up an extensive correspondence with his
friends in Poland and abroad. Nor did it prevent
him from exercising his priestly ministry among his
fellow invalids. Whether he was a patient in a sana-

torium or a prisoner in a concentration camp, he was first and foremost a priest.

All his life he carried out to the letter the solemn duty laid on Timothy: "Preach the message and, welcome or unwelcome, insist on it. Refute falsehood, correct error, call to obedience — but do all with patience and with the intention of teaching." His duty and privilege was to pass on the Good News of salvation as it had been given to him. The command was to teach all nations and in years to come he hoped to do exactly that: but first he must recover his health. In the meantime, the sanatorium at Zakopane was his world.

As soon as he was strong enough to move around, he got to work. His ministry was not always welcome. Nearby was another sanatorium called Bratnia Pomoc (Fraternal Aid) which catered for university students. It had the reputation of being godless and Kolbe soon found out that the reputation was justified. The director actively discouraged any signs of religion and most of the young patients professed themselves to be atheists, at least in public. After Kolbe's arrival things began to change, as he informed his brother, Alphonsus.

> I have begun to make short visits, one student has gone to confession, a Jew has received baptism, a number of souls are sincerely in search of the truth because they feel themselves to be unhappy without the faith; finally, there will shortly be a change in the atheistic administration.

The doctor there once called me into his office and, with the agreement of the director, asked me not to visit Bratnia Pomoc sanatorium any more. The Immaculate gave me a little strength and I answered by saying that I was a guest like anyone else and I had the right to come during visiting hours and they couldn't make any exceptions.

Other incidents are mentioned in his letters from Zakopane. For instance, he speaks of a group of forty Russian prisoners of war who spent some time there after the Red army had been defeated and driven back at the Battle of the Vistula. He befriended these strangers and enemies and managed to supply them with religious books in their own language. Before they left to return to an uncertain fate in Bolshevik Russia, he presented them all with miraculous medals. They accepted them and said, "Whenever we look at this medal, we will remember that a priest gave it to us."

Maximilian's health had improved sufficiently by the May of 1921 for him to be discharged from the sanatorium. His superiors sent him to convalesce in the quiet little town of Nieszawa where the Order had a friary. He was ordered to rest and not to involve himself in any outside work. His active spirit chafed under these restrictions but he obeyed them loyally.

In accordance with the wishes of Father Provincial, I am not doing anything here about

the M.I., I am not organising anything, even
though I am sometimes very strongly tempted.
There is a school here with about 400 children; the Catholic Youth Circle is almost non-
existent and at present confines itself to
running dances; the activity of the Third Order
is more or less defunct.

But obedience is the better way. I do what
an ordinary member of the M.I. does and
nothing more so as not to hinder my recovery.

The reference to obedience is typical of his
thought. Of the three vows which every religious
takes, poverty, chastity and obedience, he always
laid the greatest emphasis on obedience. "We
should obey the Superior," he was to say later,
"not because he is wise or experienced or prudent
or handsome or lovable but because this obedience
is the will of God and of his Blessed Mother." On
the other hand, he neither advocated nor practised
a mindless and unthinking obedience. "Obedience
does not mean that we cannot have any initiative.
We can certainly have initiative and we should not
hesitate to let our Superior know what we think or
want. But we should be just as willing to accept a
decision that goes against our natural inclinations
as one that accords with them."

He continued to take things quietly and the only
unusual apostolic activity he records is an attempt
to convert the local Protestant minister. "He would
make an excellent Franciscan," he writes optimistic-
ally, "and his church would be just perfect for

perpetual adoration of the Blessed Sacrament." His health was still improving, despite widespread rumours to the contrary. A report reached Rome in June that he had died and a Solemn Requiem Mass was sung in the International College for the repose of his soul. The rector wrote a touching obituary in the College annals: "He was an angel, a young saint, full of fervor and zeal, one of the most pious, edifying and scholastically gifted students that this college has ever had." On receiving a letter from the dead man protesting that he was still alive, the rector added the note, "He is not dead! the report was false," but allowed his testimonial to stand.

# Chapter 5
# The Knight
# of the Immaculate

It was not until the beginning of November that Maximilian was at long last allowed to return to Cracow and resume his teaching in the seminary and his direction of the M.I. Before his breakdown he had begun to organise regular meetings for the members and he was anxious to see how these were progressing. He found that the M.I. seminarians were meeting regularly under the guidance of one of the priests but that the meetings for lay people had ceased for want of leadership. He decided that the only solution was to publish a magazine which would form and guide the movement. It was to be one of the most momentous decisions of his life.

The idea of the magazine was not a new one. He had been considering it and discussing it with others for more than a year but it was not until his return to Cracow that he made the final decision to go ahead with it. Once decided, he acted with characteristic promptness and determination.

The first thing he had to do as an obedient religious was to obtain the consent of the Father Provincial. The Provincial had some doubts, principally of a financial nature, but Maximilian was well able to argue his case. Finally he got his permission but the proviso was laid down that he must finance it himself: the project was not to be a burden on the Order. He then proceeded to edit the contents, most of which he wrote himself, and to make arrangements for the printing.

The first issue appeared in January 1922. It was printed by the Cracow printing firm Czas and consisted of sixteen pages. It was intended to be a monthly but the first page carried the disarming caveat: "Due to lack of funds, we cannot guarantee regular publication of this magazine." It bore the title *Rycerz Niepokalanej* which means "The Knight of the Immaculate." Five thousand copies of this first number were printed.

As expected, finance was the biggest problem. The magazine never failed to appear on time, but there were several very close shaves. Maximilian scraped together the money for the first issue by the simple process of going out and asking people for it. But as one issue followed another, he found it next to impossible to keep up with the increasing demands of the printers. "I have just paid the printers an extra fifty per cent," he wrote to his brother, "and they have consoled me telling me that next month I will have to pay at least a further fifty per cent on top of that." It was admittedly a period of spiralling inflation but it would appear that the printers were passing on the increases with interest to their client.

Several of his biographers tell a story about a near miraculous rescue from financial ruin during this period. The printer's bill had arrived and Maximilian had exhausted all his resources. The future of the magazine seemed doomed. At his wits' end, he went into the Franciscan Church in Cracow and started to pray before the altar of Our Lady of the Seven Sorrows. As he was about to leave, he noticed an envelope on the altar. It was addressed, "To you, Immaculate Mother." He opened it and found that it contained the exact amount of money needed to pay the printer's bill. The story is a pleasing one but since we do not have Maximilian's personal testimony for it we must treat it with some caution.

The contents of the magazine were aimed at as wide a readership as possible. Maximilian was no great stylist but he had the ability to communicate effectively with a mass audience. His doctorates in philosophy and theology gave his writing a solid intellectual foundation but he managed to avoid the heaviness of most authors in these fields. Typical of the articles he wrote for *The Knight of the Immaculate* during this period is a piece called "On A Journey." It is written in dialogue form and describes a debate he had in a railway carriage. In this extract Maximilian is addressing a fellow traveller who says that the existence of God cannot be proved.

> "Do I exist?"
> "Yes."
> "And that lady and that gentleman and all of us here?"
> "Yes."
> "Are you certain?"

"Absolutely."

"How do you know?"

"Because my eyes tell me."

"And these fields and meadows which we can see from the windows of the carriage, and indeed the whole world and the stars above our heads, do they exist?"

"Yes. I admit that everything we see must exist. But God is not something that we see."

"Well then, is there an engine in front of this train?"

"Of course there is."

"Are you certain?"

"Yes."

"Can you see it?"

"No, but if it weren't there the train wouldn't be moving."

"So you admit that we can know a thing not only by seeing it directly but also by seeing the effect of which it is the cause. Isn't that so?"

"It is."

"Well then, what would you think of a man who argued this way about this watch of yours: 'This metal case has come from the gold mine of its own accord, it has melted itself down and purified itself and formed itself into its present shape by chance. The inscription was engraved on it by chance. The glass was moulded and polished by chance. Likewise the delicate wheels and springs all made themselves by chance. Finally, all the different parts were assembled together by chance and without the assistance of human mind or hand. In short, it is entirely by chance that the watch tells us the time of day.' If a man were to say this in all seriousness, what would you think about him?"

"I'd think he had taken leave of his senses."

"Well now, in nature we have organisms that are far more complex and intricate. In studying anatomy, you must have been struck by the design of the human eye, how many different parts it has, how delicate they are, how marvellously they work together to enable us to see. In the whole of nature there are millions and billions of organisms which live and grow and multiply. How could it be claimed that these marvels of nature are mere accidents? Someone might say: 'Such a thing does not happen without a cause, but its cause has another cause and that has another and so on.' But even if this series of causes could reach back into infinity, don't we have to look for some sort of First Cause? These other causes do not give any perfections from themselves but only hand down what they have already received. What we have to look for is the source of all perfections. There must be some sort of First Cause and that is God."

There is nothing original in any of the elements that make up this passage. The dialogue form goes back to Plato, the argument from causation is taken from Aristotle, the analogy of the watch comes from Paley. Thomas Aquinas provides the structure of the proof and its serene conclusion: *et hoc dicimus Deum.* What is original is the way the elements are combined and made accessible to readers unused to abstract thinking. The section on the infinite series of causes may have passed over a lot of heads, but on the whole it succeeds admirably in simplifying its argument without distorting it.

The response to the *Knight* was encouraging and demand grew steadily from issue to issue. But the continuing inflation made expansion impossible. Normally the sale of one month's issue of a magazine should pay for the printing of the next month's issue: but the value of money was now falling too fast to make this possible. All over Poland, magazines and periodicals were being forced to cease publication. The same fate was facing the *Knight.*

Maximilian could see only one solution. He must print the magazine himself. This meant buying a printing press and finding a place to operate it. The friary at Cracow was clearly not the place. The problems he had had with some of his fellow clergy there had never been fully resolved. They still looked on him and his work with suspicion and they were certainly not prepared to let him turn part of their friary into a printing works, with all the noise and dirt and confusion that would inevitably follow.

He started to look around for some friary which

might prove more welcoming. It was not easy. He had to travel the length and breadth of the country before he found what he was looking for. In the old and decaying town of Grodno in the north-east of Poland there was a similarly old and decaying friary. It was a long way from everywhere but it had plenty of spare room and the superior seemed reasonably sympathetic to the idea of the magazine. The Provincial issued an order to the effect that Father Maximilian and the editorial office of the *Knight* were to be transferred from Cracow to Grodno. On the 20th of October 1922 Maximilian arrived at the friary in Grodno with the entire editorial office in his brief-case and took up residence. It was to remain his headquarters for the next five years.

One of his first letters from Grodno was to his mother. He describes the long train journey, broken by changes at Warsaw and Bialystok. He always seemed to enjoy trains and the wide variety of travelling companions he met on them. This time he has met a friendly Jew who produced a candle for him when he had difficulty reading his breviary in the ill-lit carriage. In return, Maximilian has promised him a memento in his Mass. His room in the friary is pleasant and sunny and the apartments allotted to the magazine are big enough to hold a printing machine. He is pleased to find that the Church is dedicated to the Virgin Mary and that it contains a picture of her which is an object of widespread devotion. All in all, things seemed to augur well.

Within a few weeks he was off again, scouting for a suitable printing machine. He tried Warsaw, Lwow and Cracow and eventually found one in a convent at Lagiewniki near Cracow which he bought. He then returned to Grodno by way of Warsaw, where he purchased a supply of type.

The Provincial, who was beginning to realise that it could be useful after all for the Order to have its own printing press, gave one and a half million marks towards the expenses, and the friary at Wilno gave a further million. The amounts sound astronomical and are an indication of the way the value of the mark was plummeting. And the worst was yet to come. The January 1923 issue of the *Knight* cost 100 marks a copy, the June issue 500 marks and the December issue a staggering 20,000 marks. Things did not get under control until 1924, when a new unit of currency, the zloty, was introduced at the rate of one zloty for 1,800,000 marks.

These financial problems no longer weighed heavily on Maximilian. At the beginning of 1923 he bought enough paper to last him for the year. For the rest, he and a few Franciscan Brothers handled all the writing, editing, printing and despatching. They asked for no wages. All they needed was food and clothing and a place to sleep.

The work was not easy. Maximilian had to commute constantly between the editorial office and the rooms where the printing and binding went on. The printing machine was an antiquated model which had to be turned by hand. It was estimated that it took 70,000 turns of the big wheel to produce the 5,000 copies of the *Knight* each month. Maximilian's health was still giving cause for concern but he refused to spare himself in his eagerness to spread the ideals of the M.I. by means of the monthly magazine.

He was fortunate in his fellow-workers. Foremost among them was Brother Albert Olszakowski, who had been a printer by trade before entering the Franciscans. Brother Albert was as devoted to the work as Maximilian and as careless of his physical well-being. His premature death in 1926 was generally attributed to overwork. By that time he had trained other younger brothers in his craft and founded a tradition of dedicated workmanship that was to last long after his death.

From the beginning of 1924 the circulation of the *Knight* began to rise, first at the rate of a thousand a month, then by larger and larger amounts. By the end of the year it was 20,000, the following year 30,000, in 1926 it was 45,000 and in 1927 it reached 70,000. More and more equipment kept arriving in the friary: additional supplies of type, machines for cutting and binding, a typewriter, and last but not least a Linotype machine which took over from the old printing machine and greatly eased and speeded up the production process.

Some photographs were published showing the Brothers at work at their machines. The strange mixture of old and new seized the public imagination. Beneath the venerable vaulted ceiling of the old monastery was an array of modern machines, tended not by workers in overalls but by friars in the ancient habit of St Francis. Overlooking the whole scene was a statue of the Immaculate, surrounded by a garland of leaves and flowers. Older Catholics, including many priests, found the spectacle somewhat shocking. Maximilian pointed out that it was entirely in accordance with the practice of the past, when monks spent much of their time writing and copying manuscripts. The younger generation agreed with him and he began to receive applications from young men who were anxious to join him in his work. By 1927 he had twenty-two Brothers in the printing department in Grodno.

He continued to write much of the material himself, though always ready and indeed anxious to receive contributions from others. When his brother Alphonsus sent three articles for the magazine, Maximilian put all three into the same issue and then sent him a tongue-in-cheek apology.

> I have been guilty of some discourtesy towards you. In your letter enclosing the precious articles for the *Knight,* you suggested that I put these raisins into the cake one at a time. Actually, I put two in together and then somewhere in the course of the printing they added the third article as well. I have no idea how it happened. I think the *Knight* must have been so starving for something apart

from my own scribbles that it gobbled down
all three in one go. So the only thing you can
do is get back to your desk and write some
more.

Maximilian was now coming increasingly to rely on
Alphonsus, who had been ordained priest in 1921.
His relations with the other priests in Grodno, with
one or two exceptions, were beginning to follow
the Cracow pattern. The fault lay in the situation
rather than in any of the individuals concerned.
The friary in Grodno had taken in a cuckoo that
was fast outgrowing its nest. The printing operation was taking over more and more of the building,
not always in the most tactful manner. The
printers formed a community within a community,
whose first allegiance seemed to be to Maximilian
rather than to the friary or to the Order. Things
were becoming more and more strained. Something
had to give.

What did give, as it turned out, was Maximilian's
health. Worn out by fatigue and worry, he found
the old symptoms returning. He wrote to Alphonsus
in August 1926 to say that he was taking a month
or two's leave on doctor's orders and he hoped to
get a camera and take some photographs that
would be useful for the magazine. But the breakdown was more serious than he realised. Within a
month he was back in the sanatorium at Zakopane
with strict orders from the Father Provincial to
stay there until the doctors had declared he was
completely cured. At the same time, the Provincial

transferred Alphonsus to Grodno to take over the operation in his brother's place.

It must have been a bitter blow for Maximilian to find himself back where he started, especially at this critical juncture in his affairs. But if he felt depressed or downcast, he showed no sign of it. He was more restricted in his movements than during his previous stay and was forbidden to walk more than thirty metres from his room. He had his lungs X-rayed, apparently for the first time, and his technical mind was fascinated by this marvellous new invention. The doctors showed him the X-ray photographs and explained what they signified. The old infection had healed but there were some new affected areas. These were not large and could be cured by rest and fresh air and good food. He would have to stay the winter in the sanatorium but there was every hope that he would be given a clean bill of health in the spring.

In the meantime, he spent much of his time on the veranda, ensconced in the traditional deck-chair. The only activities left to him were praying and writing and he did both in full measure. A stream of letters went to Grodno where the unfortunate Alphonsus was overwhelmed by his new responsibilities. He had to be told everything: the manuscript for the novena was in the small book-case, the books in the top drawer were to be locked in the trunk, the key of the trunk was in the small compartment in the middle drawer. The radiator of the diesel motor was to be emptied out at night as soon as the weather began to get cold.

The cartoon of the woman in the doctor's surgery was meant to have this caption under it:

> "Doctor, do I look very pale?"
> "Yes, you do."
> "What should I do about it?"
> "Wash the powder off your face."

Among the visitors who came to Zakopane at this time was Francis, whom he had not seen for a long time. The admired eldest brother had become the black sheep of the family. He was now married with a baby daughter, but Maximilian was not sure if he had been dispensed from his religious vows before the marriage. He had no regular employment, was engaged in various murky financial activities and on one occasion narrowly escaped going to prison. Maximilian inquired about the state of his soul and received unsatisfactory replies. Then he went off again, borrowing twenty zloties for his train fare. Maximilian asked Alphonsus to pray for him but to be careful about giving him money. There is no doubt that he felt in some way guilty over the fact that Francis had left the Order to join the army thirteen years before.

In December Brother Albert died of typhus and Maximilian went to Grodno for his funeral. It is not clear how he managed to get the doctor's permission to make this long and tiring winter journey, if indeed he did get his permission. It was a rather distressing visit. Not only was the head printer dead, but one of his best assistants, Brother

Evaristus, had just been diagnosed as infected by tuberculosis and several of the others were showing worrying symptoms as well. Fresh from the airy antiseptic wards of the sanatorium, Maximilian was very conscious of the cramped conditions under which the Brothers were working and of the way they were spreading germs from one to the other in the old and badly ventilated building. He became more convinced than ever that a change would have to be made and made soon.

Back in Zakopane in January, he received a severe and well-deserved rebuke from the Provincial and wrote to tell Alphonsus about it.

> I wrote to tell Father Provincial what the doctor had said, namely that I could either go back to work at once and complete my recovery in Grodno, or else that I could spend the winter here. He answered that I was to stay in Zakopane until April, or even longer if the doctor thought that was too short. He also said that I was not to go on any journeys or involve myself in any kind of business. As a result, I'm not going to give you any more advice or make any more decisions for you, because that is the will of the Immaculate. If I did anything against her will, I would certainly be in the wrong. So you will have to rely on the Immaculate for guidance.

He was as good as his word. During February and March he sat patiently in his deckchair on the veranda, breathing the cold mountain air into his tattered lungs. To all of Alphonsus's anxious queries he gave the same answer: the Immaculate will guide you. He was prepared to disobey his doctor but not his religious superior.

His reward came in April when he was finally declared to be cured. The doctor told him that he must take good care of himself in the future, sleep ten hours a night, spend four hours every day in the open air, make sure his room was always dry and sunny, eat well and avoid lifting heavy weights with his right arm. How well he carried out these instructions we do not know. But after this there was to be no serious recurrence of the disease, despite a range of activities that would tax the strength of the healthiest man.

He arrived back in Grodno in mid-April. The winter snows had melted, the days had lengthened, spring was in the air. He knew it was only to be for a short while. He had every confidence that the Immaculate would solve the problem. His confidence was not misplaced. A few weeks after his return he met a priest from a neighboring parish who told him about a piece of land that might be available for his purpose. It was situated at a place called Teresin in the very center of Poland, beside the main railway line and only about twenty-five miles from the capital city of Warsaw. It was exactly what he had been looking for.

# Chapter 6
# Niepokalanow

Everything up to this had been a kind of apprenticeship. It was just ten years since that Roman summer when he confided to his friends his plans for the Militia of the Immaculate and suffered his first haemorrhage. Those ten years had been years of pain and heartbreak, physical and mental suffering, misunderstanding, frustration, betrayal. It had been a time of trial but also a time of learning. He was no longer the naive and idealistic seminarian with a simplistic master-plan for the salvation of the world. It was not that his zeal had lessened or that his trust in God and his Blessed Mother had grown any less strong. But he knew now much more clearly the kind of obstacles he had to face, in himself and others. He knew that obedience did not exclude initiative and that dependence on divine grace did not mean a passive and fatalistic acceptance of the course of events. Consciously or unconsciously, he was beginning to make fuller use of his gifts: his organising skill, his qualities of leadership, his far-ranging vision, his ability to analyse and respond to the spirit of the age. The apprenticeship was over. The master period was about to begin. He was thirty-three years old.

The months of July and August were months of

hectic activity. He travelled back and forth across the country, campaigning on two fronts. He had to persuade the owner of the land to offer it to the Order. He had to persuade the Order to accept.

The owner of the land was a wealthy and pious nobleman, Prince John Drucki Lubecki, who was sympathetic to the Franciscans in general and to the work of the M.I. in particular. Maximilian had discussions first with the Prince's agent and then with the Prince himself, and the result was that the Prince agreed to make a free donation of the land. The only recompense he asked was that the friars should promise in perpetuity to offer twenty-six Masses a year for his intentions, two of them to be celebrated in his palace.

Next, Maximilian had to get the consent of the Order. The Provincial Chapter of the Order was meeting at the time, consisting of delegates from all the houses of the Conventual Franciscans in Poland. Their feelings must have been mixed. On the one hand, they recognised the value of the publications being issued by Maximilian and they realised that if he were to continue and expand the work he would have to find new premises. On the other hand, if he were to be allowed to set up on his own, it would mean giving a position of considerable power and authority to a young man with a rather erratic track record. Their decision was curious: they accepted the Prince's offer but rejected the stipulations about the Masses which he had laid down.

While matters were at this impasse, Maximilian

made a bold and characteristic gesture. On the 6th of August, 1927, he arrived at Teresin with a statue of the Immaculate, set it up on a little pedestal in the middle of the fields and solemnly blessed it. A photograph of the event shows a small group around the statue, clergy mingling with local farming people, the men in their good suits, the women in headscarves and floral dresses. In the middle, Maximilian is shepherding a group of children, including a tiny flower-girl in a snow-white dress. Around them the level fields stretch away to the horizon.

It has not been unknown in various places and at various times for nuns to throw miraculous medals over the walls of properties which they hoped to acquire. Maximilian's move was of a similar but rather more public nature. It could have caused resentment on one side or the other, as a high-handed effort to pre-empt the negotations. But Maximilian was confident that the Immaculate would now take the place under her protection and make sure that all difficulties were smoothed away: and so it happened. On the 1st of September the Prince agreed to withdraw his stipulations and to make over the land unconditionally to the Order. The successor of that statue still stands today in the same place.

Maximilian was now master of Teresin, which consisted of a number of empty fields and a statue. Before he could start any building he had to get permission from Rome, which did not arrive until the end of September. The Polish winter was approaching and it looked as though no move could be made until the spring. Once again Maximilian made a bold decision. He made arrangements with the railway company to start transporting the printing presses from Grodno on the 7th of November. He would have a place ready to receive them by then.

A group of Brothers came from Grodno to join him and work started on the site at Teresin at the beginning of October. The place now had a new name, Niepokalanow, which had been suggested by the Provincial. The name comes from the Polish word *niepokalana,* meaning immaculate. The usual English translation of Niepokalanow is City of the Immaculate.

Any kind of architectural pretension was out of the question. All they could hope to do was to provide shelter of the simplest sort for men and machines. The neighbors were helpful. One man gave them a place to sleep, others provided food. A benefactor sent four wagon-loads of planks, another three hundred sheets of plywood.

They worked frantically against their deadline. The buildings were made of wood and roofed with a kind of tarred felt. Holes were left where the windows could later be fitted. There were no floors other than the levelled and beaten earth. Planks were used for tables and boxes for chairs. It was the kind of poverty of which St Francis would have approved.

The transfer of the machines took place in mid-November as planned. Local farmers provided wagons to bring them from the station to the new monastery. Before the end of the month, Niepokalanow was in full swing. The printing presses were rolling out the *Knight* and other publications. The chapel was in use for daily worship: the first Mass had been said there on the 12th of November. The community had taken up residence in their primitive new quarters, eighteen Brothers and two priests, Maximilian and Alphonsus Kolbe. And all this in what had been open fields less than two months before.

They prepared themselves for a long hard winter. A young man who applied to join the community at this time was warned by Maximilian to bring plenty of clothes if he did not wish to freeze during the cold weather. "Also bring bed linen and some money for your return journey in case you find it too difficult to adapt to our kind of religious life. But there are many who have adapted and are happy; and you too, with the help of the Immaculate, can become a fervent religious." The wind whistled around their ears as they lay in bed at night. The water was frozen in their basins when they rose in the morning. But they were happy.

As time went on, conditions in Niepokalanow improved, but they have remained simple and spartan to this day. Maximilian knew from his own experience that the workers needed adequate food and housing but he saw no need for any kind of ostentation. Whatever money came in was to be used to extend the scope of their apostolate. "We may live in huts ourselves," he said, "but the word

which moulds the human spirit must be printed on
the most modern machinery and made as widely
and easily available as possible." He himself was
full of plans for the expansion of the publishing
work, magazines for various interests, foreign language editions, books and pamphlets on religious
subjects, even a daily newspaper. It would take
time and money but with the help of the Immaculate it would all come to pass some day.

The most urgent need at the moment was not
time or money but personnel. In order to expand
the work, more Brothers were needed. He had no
shortage of applicants but he was under orders to
restrict the number he accepted, perhaps because
he was still not entirely trusted by the other priests
of the Province. In February 1929 the circulation
of the *Knight* reached 100,000 and he wrote to the
Provincial to ask that the restrictions on new
entrants be removed. The letter gives a vivid
picture of the organisation of Niepokalanow at the
time.

> Given our present circulation, if the work is
> to run smoothly without going on too late at
> night or being done in too much of a rush, the
> office staff must have one Brother for every
> 10,000 copies of the *Knight*, that is, ten plus
> a director, total: 11. The despatch depart-
> ment needs one for every 20,000, making 5
> (adding the aforementioned: 16). The type-
> setting department needs at least six (adding
> the others: 22); each of the large machines

needs two (in the Warsaw printers they have three for every machine, though their speed is 30% slower), that is 4 x 2 = 8, then one for the treadle machine and a director, making ten in all (plus the others: 32); the binding department needs two for the stitching machine, two for the folding machine and one for the cutting machine, that is, 5 (plus the others: 37); in the maintenance and repair shop, given the fact that we bought old machines cheaply and that they need repair, at least three (with the foregoing: 40). At least 12 for the building work, since we do everything ourselves, from the lowest job (such as carrying building materials) to the most demanding; five for the carpenter's shop, to make doors, windows and furniture (total: 57). Then one to help in the management, one in the editing, and one to be combined sacristan and porter and to make the cinctures (total: 60). Finally, to provide for food and clothing, that is, to look after the vegetable garden, the receipt of donations, the larder, the kitchen, the store-room, the tailoring, the laundry, the shoemakers: about 15, allowing a proportion of 1 to 4 (total: 75).

He goes on to point out that these figures represent a bare minimum if the Brothers are to go about their work "calmly, without nervous pressure or hurry, without shortening their time for meditation, recreation and sleep, and in such a way that everything is done as well as possible and in accordance with the religious spirit." He ends by mentioning how undermanned the carpentry section is: they still have not put in double windows and they are so short of furniture that they have to put their basins on the floor when they are washing.

The request was granted and Maximilian was allowed to appeal in the *Knight* for vocations to the brotherhood. He was also given permission to go ahead with another project, that of opening a minor seminary in Niepokalanow to educate future priests for the foreign missions. From the beginning, he had seen his apostolate as being directed not just to Poland but to the whole world. Now he was in a position to start doing something practical about it. The minor seminary was to be a boarding college on the lines of the one he had attended in Lwow: boys who believed they were called to be missionary priests could come there to complete their general education in a religious environment before going on to a major seminary for their studies in philosophy and theology. This too was advertised in the *Knight* and opened in September 1929.

Just two years had passed since the first planks had been nailed together on the site of the new monastery at Teresin. The growth had been spectacular. The community had increased fivefold. Now, in addition to the two Father Kolbes, there were sixty-seven Brothers or candidates for the Brotherhood and 33 boys in the minor seminary. The circulation of the *Knight* was still rising, other publications were in course of production, new buildings and machines were being constantly added to the complex. Niepokalanow was no longer a delicate seedling but a sturdy plant. An era of consolidation and peaceful growth lay ahead.

Maximilian chose this moment to make another dramatic move, his boldest yet. He felt that he could safely leave Niepokalanow to develop along the lines he had laid down while he himself went off to spread the message of the gospel through the world outside. He announced his intention of setting out for the Far East and of founding Cities of the Immaculate in the countries of Asia and he asked for volunteers to accompany him. To those who protested that the young monastery could not afford to lose some of its best blood, he answered that missionary work would strengthen rather than weaken the community. "St Francis had only a tiny group," he said, "but he was the first to venture on missionary activity at a time when other larger Orders were not even thinking about it."

He obtained approval from the Provincial, who by this time seemed to have lost the ability to say no to him any more. He also had to get permission from the Superior General of the Order and he decided to travel to Rome for this purpose. On the journey he visited some monasteries and his comments show where his interest lay. "I have been to visit St Gabriel's in Mödling. It is the monastery of the Divine Word Fathers, magnificently built and planned, not in the sense of useless decoration but because of the intelligent way the various sections are laid out. Typographical machines, offset machines, binding machines — in fact, machines everywhere."

He arrived in Rome on the 18th of January 1930. There, in addition to obtaining the General's authorization, he made inquiries about opportunities for spreading the M.I. and the *Knight* in the Far East. In India, there seemed to be possibilities in both Bombay and Calcutta. In China, the Bishop of Shanghai had given the Franciscans permission to work in his diocese, a permission which they had not yet made us of. In Japan the Bishop of Nagasaki was known to be anxious to have the help of more priests and religious in that city. There were plenty of openings. The sooner they got going the better.

He headed for Marseilles where he booked passages for Shanghai for himself and the four Brothers who were to accompany him. He booked third class, the cheapest, and succeeded in getting a twenty per cent reduction. He wrote to Niepokalanow to tell them to start preparing at once. "Our missionaries can stop shaving because they will have to wear beards in the East — I am told that it's the custom out there."

It was his first visit to France and he took the opportunity to visit some of the shrines that had special associations for him. From Lourdes he sent a picture postcard of the Basilica. "The Basilica is graceful but it is made by the hands of men. In the Grotto, on the other hand, we see the work of the Immaculate and it is a place of prayer without ceasing."

Then he made for Paris and, as soon as he arrived, took a taxi to the Convent of the Miraculous Medal in the Rue du Bac. Unused to the ways of Paris taxi-drivers, he paid the fare on the meter, then instead of a tip gave the driver a miraculous medal. The infuriated man threw it on the ground and stamped on it. His visit to Lisieux was more pleasant. He saw the home and convent of St Thérèse, patroness of the foreign missions and one of his favorite saints. He was pleased to find among her childish playthings a chess set — a game he was fond of himself. Then he headed back to Niepokalanow with less than a month to make his final preparations.

It was arranged that the faithful Alphonsus would take over as superior when he left. The four Brothers who were to go with him were Zeno Zebrowski, Hilary Lysakowski, Sigmund Krol and Severinus Dagis. A photograph was taken of the five before their departure from the monastery. Maximilian is in the middle, looking very seriously at the camera through the steel-rimmed spectacles he had been wearing since student days. He is a lightly built man of below average height with a couple of weeks' growth of beard upon his face. He is just thirty-six years of age.

They left Niepokalanow on the 26th of February and went first to Rome where they were received by the Pope and photographed again, this time in the Colosseum. Then they made their way to Marseilles where they boarded their ship, the

*Angers.* At 4 p.m. on the 7th of March they set sail for the East.

# Chapter 7
# The Japanese Mission

To the modern mind, the five travellers would seem to have been quite exceptionally ill-prepared for the journey. In those days missionaries did not undergo the rigorous training and orientation that are considered essential today: it was time enough to start learning the local language and customs when they arrived at their destination. But these five were not even clear what their destination was. All they knew was that they were going to build cities and publish writings for the glory of God and the salvation of souls. They hoped to be in Shanghai in mid-April, which would give them two weeks before the beginning of May, traditionally the month of Mary. It would be very fitting if they could honour her during that month by publishing the first issue of the *Knight* in Chinese or Japanese or both. The fact that they knew not a word of either of these languages did not bother them at all. If the Immaculate wanted it, it would come to pass.

Life on board the *Angers* passed quietly and uneventfully. To their pleased surprise, they were allotted a second class cabin at no extra charge. They ate in the third class but this was no hardship for those accustomed to Niepokalanow diet. "The food in third class is plentiful and excellent," wrote Maximilian and added in wonder, "We eat four times a day." He celebrated Mass each morning in the first class music salon for his little flock.

The boat stopped at Port Said, Singapore and Saigon. At each place Maximilian went to see the local Bishop and explore the publishing possibilities. He was received well everywhere, especially in Saigon, where some of the native priests offered to help with the work. He promised to send two Brothers within six months to start the publication of the *Knight.*

After leaving Saigon, the boat headed north into the cooler waters of the China Sea, greatly to the relief of Maximilian who had found it difficult to sleep or even to breathe in the heat of the tropics. At Hong Kong, he inspected the printing establishment run by the Salesians of Don Bosco. Then the boat continued on to its destination, Shanghai, where the passengers disembarked on the 11th of April, 1930

Shanghai was to prove a bitter disappointment. At first, everything seemed to be going well. Maximilian was warmly welcomed by the Bishop and given permission to distribute a Chinese edition of the *Knight.* He went looking for suitable premises and was fortunate to come into contact with a wealthy Catholic layman, Lo Pa Hong, who undertook to provide a suitable house for the project at his own expense. The blow fell when Maximilian discovered that permission to distribute the *Knight* did not include permission to print it. He wrote to the General in Rome.

> As I anticipated before I left Poland, there are great difficulties about the magazine, but they don't come from the pagans, they come from the European missionaries. China is divided out into territories for the different religious Orders and Congregations and they alone have the right to work in their own territory. We could print the magazine in Shensi, where we have our own mission, but it has no means of communication by rail or river.

After ten days of frantic but fruitless negotiations, Maximilian decided to cut his losses and try Japan. Leaving Brothers Zeno and Sigmund behind in Shanghai in the hope of an improvement in the situation, he set sail for Nagasaki with the other two and arrived there on the 24th of April, exhausted and discouraged, a stranger in a strange land.

One month later, to the very day, the community at Niepokalanow were astonished to receive a triumphant telegram.

> NAGASAKI 24 V 1930. JAPANESE KNIGHT PUBLISHED TODAY. WE HAVE PRINTING PRESS. PRAISE THE IMMACULATE.
> MAXIMILIAN.

The steps by which the magazine was produced in thirty days were all human but the result still seems little short of miraculous. Maximilian's crucial first meeting with the Bishop of Nagasaki was the key to his success. The city of Nagasaki was the centre of Catholicism in the country. About 50,000 Catholics were living there at the time, more than half of the Catholic population of Japan. They had kept the faith through centuries of savage persecution and could count many martyrs among their forebears. Among these were Father Paul Miki and his companions who were put to death in Nagasaki in 1597 and canonised in 1862.

Bishop Hayasaka greeted Maximilian as an answer to prayer. He had in his diocese the major seminary where most Japanese priests were educated and was having difficulty in finding teaching staff. In particular, he was looking for someone to take the chair of philosophy. The unexpected arrival of a doctor of philosophy seemed like a god-send. An agreement was quickly made between the two. Maximilian undertook to take on the position of professor of philosophy in the seminary. In return, the Bishop gave him permission to found a mission and to publish his magazine.

Maximilian had not come to the Far East in order to teach philosophy, but he soon found that the arrangement had its advantages. He rented a room near the seminary and started his lectures at once. He knew as little Japanese as his students knew Polish, but they had in common the Latin language which was the medium of teaching in all Catholic seminaries at that time. His work gave him an immediate entry into the intellectual life of

Catholic Japan and he used it to good effect.

His first step was to write out all the articles for the first issue of the *Knight* in Latin and then hand them over to some of the native clergy for translation. Then he set about getting it printed. He was determined to have his own printing press but he realised that it would take time to buy the necessary machinery and learn how to use it, so he made arrangements with a local printing firm to print the first issue. While the printing was going on, he heard of a printing press for sale in the city of Osaka. He went to see it and bought it at once for 650 yen. Along with it he bought a supply of Japanese characters for the printing, 145,000 in all, for a further 400 yen. Having made arrangements for it to be transported, he rushed back to Nagasaki in time to see the first copies of the magazine coming off the press. Ten thousand copies of the first number were printed, an ambitious venture in a country with less than a hundred thousand Catholics. It was called *Mugenzai no Seibo no Kishi*, the Knight of the Immaculate.

One Japanese witness said during Maximilian's beatification process: "It is hardly possible to imagine how the magazine *Mugenzai no Seibo no Kishi* could have been published by purely human means, without any knowledge of the language, without any editorial premises, and without any money." Anyone who has had the slightest experience of dealing with the problems of printing and publishing will appreciate these words. For Maximilian the explanation was simple. Sending some copies of the *Kishi* to the two Brothers in Shanghai he wrote: "The month of May has been full of favors granted by the Immaculate."

In June he returned to Poland for the Provincial Chapter, held every three years. Since he had little luggage to transport this time, he travelled by the trans-Siberian railroad, much faster than the boat. On the way he visited Shanghai where he found the situation unchanged and directed the two Brothers there to join the others in Nagasaki. Arrived in Poland, he reported to the Provincial Chapter on the latest state of events and was authorised to found a City of the Immaculate in Nagasaki. Then he returned to Japan, again travelling by rail and taking with him two Polish seminarians to complete their studies for the priesthood in Japan. The reasons he gave for taking them are interesting and show how quick he was to size up the situation in that country and to adapt his strategy accordingly.

> If they go now, after a quick course in minor logic and some ethics, to join the Japanese seminarians and study along with them, then as well as their sacred studies they will gain a good command of the Japanese language and a knowledge and insight into the habits, customs, defects and qualities of the Japanese people. They will get to know and make friends with their future fellow workers in the religious field. Apart from everything else, they will be able to learn the theory and prac-

tice of editing the *Kishi* in accordance with local needs and of directing the editorial complex.

Then after six years' preparation, they will be fully ready to roll up their sleeves, with all the theoretical and practical knowledge needed for their particular mission — not to mention all the Japanese books they will have read by that time.

But if they are already priests when they arrive, instead of getting down to work, they will have to start learning the language, which needs at least three years' study! Moreover, the memory of a priest is not as good as that of a seminarian. As regards knowledge of local conditions, a Salesian who came to Japan as a priest three years ago told me that the more he studies a Japanese the less he understands him. Yes, it is not easy to get to the bottom of the Asiatic character.

At the end of August Maximilian arrived back in Nagasaki with the two students to find that he had been let down not only by the inscrutable orientals but by his own Polish Brothers as well. In his absence, the *Kishi* had come to a halt and no issue had been printed for August even though all the copy had been prepared. However, everything was changed by his return and the issue of a double number for August/September restored things to normal.

For October he printed 18,000 copies, for

November 20,000 and for December, "the month of the Immaculate, "he printed 25,000. A Methodist scholar, Professor Yamaki, volunteered to help with the work of translating the articles into Japanese and also presented the community with a roast chicken, which they gladly devoured. The food was in general something of a problem. "We don't drink milk," he wrote, "because it is too dear (I haven't seen a single cow in Japan), we can't even think of meat and it isn't possible to eat other foods because they are not for European stomachs: so we eat rice, pearl barley, foods made with flour, and then more rice and more pearl barley . . ." The approach of winter with its rain and cold north winds had an adverse effect on his lungs; but in spite of everything he and the little community remained busy and cheerful.

They prepared for the Feast of the Immaculate Conception, the 8th of December, by nine days of prayer. On the day before the Feast, just after Mass, a telegram arrived for Maximilian. It was from Niepokalanow and it read, "Alphonsus died holy death. Everything as before. Florian."

It was two weeks before letters arrived giving further details. Father Alphonsus's death had been totally unexpected. Towards the end of November he had complained of feeling unwell. His condition rapidly worsened and acute appendicitis was diagnosed. He was rushed to a hospital in Warsaw but died before the surgeons could operate. He was thirty-four years old. He had been closer to Maximilian than any other living being, a friend as well as a brother, patient, loyal, devoted and utterly reliable. Earlier that year, with some kind of premonition, Maximilian had written to him, "I have been worried for some time with the thought that the life is too hard for you and that you may fall sick as a result, but I have entrusted this worry to the Immaculate." Now the Immaculate had taken him to herself.

The Mass on the 8th of December was offered for the repose of his soul. Maximilian said it in the little chapel of their house, wearing the white vestments of the Feastday, while the Brothers sang hymns in honor of the Immaculate. After the first shock, he had felt a sense of peace and consolation. "He is really to be envied," he wrote to his mother: "it was for the Immaculate that he lived and suffered and worked and wore himself out, and she has taken him to be with her in the days of preparation for her Feast." Nonetheless, the death of Alphonsus left a void in his life that no one else was ever able to fill.

There was something else that was causing him disquiet. The future of Niepokalanow now seemed to him to be in danger. He knew there were still many priests in the Polish province who looked on the monastery with disfavor and would be happy to see its wings clipped: he called them the "Cracovians" in memory of his unhappy days in the friary at Cracow. A new superior might be appointed who would run down the publishing operation and allow the place to revert to the more traditional pattern. The words "everything as before" in the telegram from Father Florian had been intended to reassure him but it was not until fuller news arrived from Poland that his mind was set at rest. Father Florian Koziura had joined Alphonsus at Niepokalanow a couple of months earlier and after the latter's death he was at once appointed to take over as superior of the monastery. He proved to be a capable and energetic administrator and under his leadership the work went ahead in full accord with Maximilian's vision.

# Chapter 8
# The Garden
# of the Immaculate

The overcrowding in the rented house in Nagasaki was becoming intolerable. There were seven Poles in the community along with a number of Japanese who were aspiring to join the Order or helping with the work. The printing operation was making increasing inroads on their living space. Every available corner was filled with printing machinery, boxes of type, bales of paper, stacks of magazines. On top of everything else, four more Franciscans were on their way to join them from Niepokalanow. Maximilian had to find somewhere fast.

The four newcomers — a priest, a Brother and two seminarians — travelled in March by the Siberian railway. Maximilian sent them detailed instructions based on his own experiences and they give an interesting sidelight on how to make a nine-day train journey across the Soviet Union in the nineteen-thirties. He told them to wear lay clothes and to take with them tea, sugar, biscuits, tinned food, cups, spoons and two tea-pots: a large one for getting the boiling water (available at all stations in an urn marked "Kipiatok" in Russian letters) and a small one for making the tea in. At night, they are given full instructions on how to arrange the couchettes for sleep and a warning to lock and wedge the door against unwanted visitors. In the morning, they are to rise early so that they can say their prayers and also avoid the long queue that forms outside the wash-room (they mustn't forget to bring toilet paper with them).

They are to be careful what they say in front of strangers and they should ask their Polish fellow-travellers not to reveal their identity: but if questioned directly by anyone in authority they are to say that they are missionaries bound for Japan. Once they cross the border into Manchuria they can relax. "Then at last you can put on the beloved religious habit. At Harbin the train stops for half an hour. We rushed off like a bullet in a car to a church, I gave Holy Communion to the Brothers and received myself, and then we rushed back again in the car. But it's a risk and since you don't know the city of Harbin you'd better not chance it." Then on to the port of Pusan in Korea where they board the ship for Japan.

The four arrived safely in Nagasaki at the end of March to find that Maximilian had just bought the ground for his Japanese Niepokalanow. It was situated on the side of a steep hill in the suburb of Hongochi. Its distance from the center of the city was an inconvenience but it meant that Maximilian was able to buy an extensive site for 7,000 yen, far less than he would have had to pay for a smaller site in the city itself.

He started to build at once. The first building was a simple one-storeyed affair, with walls of ill-fitting planks through whose gaps winds blew and noxious insects entered. The kitchen consisted of an iron stove in the open air. "But we are full of joy because our Niepokalanow is at last a reality and we have Jesus with us in our little chapel." He was unable to find a suitable Japanese translation of City of the Immaculate. He eventually settled on the title Mugenzai no Sono, which means Garden of the Immaculate and has about it a charming and authentically Japanese delicacy.

Most of the money came from Poland. He published appeals for funds in the Polish *Knight* and they drew a generous response. The new superior of Niepokalanow, Father Florian, proved himself a reliable ally. He himself was in dire financial straits having just bought a new rotary printing press for the monastery and one of his replies to Maximilian's begging letters begins with the words, "Help! Help! This is too much!" But he was always ready to respond to his appeals for money and men to the utmost of his ability. It was money gathered through the Polish *Knight* that paid for the land and the first building and enabled Maximilian to continue expanding the scope of his work all through his six years in Japan.

There were other worries too. As in Poland and in China, some of his worst problems were caused by his fellow clergy. Some of his own community were growing homesick for Poland and complaining about the work and the conditions. One of them, Father Constantius, was writing letters to the head house in Rome attacking Maximilian and accusing him of planning to set up a breakaway religious

Order of his own. Some of the older missionaries from the other Orders also looked unfavorably on this new arrival with his flair for publicity and his high-pressure approach to evangelisation.

Maximilian did not disdain the traditional missionary methods. He and his community had many individual conversions to their credit and also succeeded in attracting a steady flow of native vocations to their Order. But Maximilian saw clearly that it was not enough to work for individual conversions in a country of eighty million people where less than 100,000 were Catholics. He wanted to reach out to all those millions he could never meet as individuals, to influence their whole pattern of thought and culture and to make Christian ideals and values part of the national consciousness.

It was for this reason that he kept pushing up the circulation of *Mugenzai no Seibo no Kishi* far beyond what was needed by the Catholic population. In a comparatively short time it surpassed the sales of all the other Catholic publications and began to be read increasingly by those of other faiths. At first the articles in the magazine were somewhat pious and sentimental in style but gradually, following the recommendations of Bishop Hayasaka, Maximilian adopted a more reasoned and intellectual approach, suited to a country with one of the oldest civilizations in the world. In modern times missionaries use the term "preevangelization," meaning the need to prepare the soil for the reception of Christianity before the actual work of conversion can begin. Maximilian did not know the term but he understood the reality long before most of his fellow missionaries.

During all the other activities of this period, Maximilian continued to teach philosophy in the seminary of Nagasaki, now a considerable distance away since the move to Mugenzai no Sono. In a letter to a missionary magazine he described what this entailed.

> After morning meditation, Holy Mass, Divine Office and breakfast, I have to be ready to leave our mountain village immediately for the twenty minutes' walk to the tram stop. The journey continues more comfortably then and after two changes of tram I arrive at the diocesan seminary where I have to stuff the brains of the almond-eyed philosophers with definitions, divisions, theses and the like. And then the return journey. On the tram the heat is not too bad, but after the last tram stop I have to climb uphill and, even though it is a good wide road, what with the noise of bicycle bells and motor horns and the roar of traffic and the heat of the sun, I lose whatever little strength I have left in my legs and have to drag myself along.

The writing of letters like this was just one more of the burdens he had to shoulder. Many of them still survive, artless, humorous, vivid. He seems incapable of planning a letter in advance and puts down the thoughts as they come to him. He almost always has to add a postscript, which is sometimes longer and more interesting than the letter itself. A notable instance of this is the letter he wrote to the Polish Provincial, Father Cornelius Czupryk, in December 1931.

The main part of the letter is dated the 12th of December and describes various problems within his community. That very day, for instance, their only Japanese member, Brother Marian, had reached a crisis in his vocation and walked out of the monastery: two hours later he was back again begging to be re-admitted, having changed his mind at the tram stop. The first postscript, written at 10.30 on the evening of the same day, conveys a request from the community for two more Brothers to be sent out from Poland.

The next postscript was written the following day. "Last night and again today there has been a snow-storm. Some fell on my face so that I had to cover my head in order to sleep. The Brothers' eiderdowns are white (they sleep in the attic) and the water in their wash-basins is mixed with snow. They were joking about it at breakfast but I am a little worried about our health. I think the present building is in urgent need of extensions and this would cost at least 2,000 zloties (that is, 400 yen)."

The next postscript is dated the 15th of December. In the meantime he had posted the letter but the post office had sent it back because they were unable to read the address. Then follow two more, dated the 16th of December. The first acknowledges a telegram from Niepokalanow, the second adds offhandedly some news about his own health:

> For some time past I have been suffering from abscesses. As soon as one grows and bursts, another begins to appear. Today one of the Brothers had to support me during Mass, and because my temperature has gone up (though not very much) I am finding it difficult to work. Still it's not anything serious, except that the abscesses are painful until they burst. On two occasions the doctor has lanced them for me but this hasn't stopped others from appearing. Maybe they are caused by bacilli. Praise the Immaculate!

One of the doctors who attended him in Japan, Dr. Paul Nagai Takashi, later testified: "His life was one long act of heroism. I examined him and found that one of his lungs was badly diseased. I prescribed absolute rest but he said that he would keep on working because he had been in that condition for years. He had a will to survive that I found truly extraordinary."

During the new year, Maximilian's thoughts kept returning to the countless millions in other parts of Asia who had never heard the name of Christ. He wrote to the Polish Provincial in the name of all the members of Mugenzai no Sono and asked permission for them to take a fourth vow in addition to the customary three vows of poverty, chastity and obedience. This was to be a vow declaring that they were ready to go for the love of the Immaculate to any mission however arduous and even to death itself. The rule of St Francis stated that no-one could be sent to the missions unless he volunteered to do so. By this vow they would volunteer permanently to undertake any missionary work in any place if asked by their superior. The Provincial gave his permission and the community took the fourth vow on the 25th of March 1932.

He also obtained permission from the Provincial (since Mugenzai no Sono was still regarded as the responsibility of the Polish Province) to investigate the possibility of setting up Cities of the Immaculate in other parts of Asia. A great deal of his limited time and even more limited strength was to be spent in a laborious and ultimately unsuccessful attempt to carry out this ambition.

His own inclination was to try China once again but the Provincial suggested that India might offer a more promising prospect. Obedient as ever, he set off for India at the end of May, calling at Singapore and Colombo before ending up at Ernakulam on the Malabar coast of India.

In Ernakulam he met an unfamiliar variant of a familiar problem. He was accustomed to finding that the Church authorities caused him more trouble than the pagans, but he had never before encountered a situation where there were two different Church authorities. Ernakulam had two Archbishops, one a Spaniard serving the Catholics of the Latin or Western rite, the other an

Indian serving the Catholics of the Syro-Malabar rite. Through a chance meeting with a priest on the train, he went to see the Syro-Malabar Archbishop instead of the Latin one and the resulting complications took all his tact and patience to unravel.

While he was waiting in the corridor for an interview with the Latin Archbishop, an incident occurred which seemed to him a good omen. In the corridor was a statue of his beloved St Thérèse with a vase of flowers in front of it. He asked the saint to sort out the problem and immediately one of the flowers fell down on to the pedestal. He took this as a sign that his prayer had been heard.

After this, the difficulties seemed to melt away. The Latin Archbishop drove him around in his own car to look at various sites and finally agreed to make him a gift of a house and a piece of land in a place called Amalam close to the city and the railway. Joyfully he sent off a telegram to Niepokalanow: "Inform Provincial: Amalam Indian Niepokalanow founded. Praise the Immaculate. Maximilian." He then left Ernakulam, intending to send a group of Brothers there as soon as possible, and arrived back in Nagasaki towards the end of July.

Both his joy and his telegram proved to be premature. The Provincial seems to have been personally in favour of the Indian project but he had to take account both of the scarcity of Brothers available and suitable for the work and of the continuing opposition to Maximilian and his ideas within the Province. He decided to refer a final decision on the matter to the next Provincial Chapter which was due to meet the following summer.

By this time, Maximilian had come to dread the three-yearly ordeal of the Provincial Chapter. He was due to attend the 1933 Chapter as the representative of Mugenzai no Sono and he foresaw an uphill battle in defence not only of the Japanese and Indian projects but of the Polish Niepokalanow as well.

Letters coming from Poland were not reassuring. One said that "extremely important decisions are going to be made regarding Niepokalanow." Another said "not all the Fathers of the Province are convinced that our life here is truly Franciscan or that it has much of a future." The Provincial himself wrote to warn him that he should prepare himself for storms ahead.

In fairness it must be said that the dissenters were not motivated simply by jealousy of Maximilian's achievements. They genuinely felt that he was departing from the traditional spirit of the Order by the unusual austerity of life that he advocated in his monasteries and by his teaching regarding the Blessed Virgin. They thought that his constant invocation of the Immaculate showed a lack of theological balance and that he seemed at times to be putting Mary in the place of God. In particular, his advocacy of the fourth vow must have appeared an unwarranted and potentially divisive action. The Order had flourished for seven hundred years with the same three vows: what was the need of a fourth?

# Chapter 9
# Humiliation

It was in a somewhat sombre mood that Maximilian left Nagasaki for Poland in April 1933. He was not made any more cheerful by the fact that the man who was to take charge of Mugenzai no Sono in his absence was Father Constantius, who still showed little enthusiasm for the M.I. or the *Kishi*. He travelled by the Italian ship *Conte Rosso*, as the political situation made the overland route inadvisable. As the boat drew away from the land, he watched the group of friars on the dockside growing smaller and smaller until they could be seen no longer. He consoled himself with the thought that the two Poles who had landed with him three years ago had now become twelve and that their first Japanese Brother (the one who had changed his mind at the tram stop) had just taken his simple vows.

On his way he spent three weeks in Rome, where he met and discussed his plans with the Superior General of the Order. Then he continued on to Poland and made at once for Niepokalanow, which he had not seen for three years. It had expanded greatly since then in the number of its buildings and personnel and in the scope of its activities. Father John Burdyszek, who was a young seminarian there at the time, describes the occasion in his valuable memoir *Father Maximilian Kolbe: Fire Enkindled.*

> I well remember that day at the end of May when we welcomed him back to Niepokalanow. We young seminarians were very excited to see in the flesh our missionary with the long beard, about whom we had heard so much. It was a great occasion for us. The day itself was glorious. The sun had shone from quite early in the morning. Father Maximilian offered his thanksgiving Mass in the chapel he himself had helped to build. All the inhabitants of the City of Mary Immaculate, over four hundred, gathered together before the statue of the Immaculate Virgin outside the refectory. I could hardly hear his voice among the crowd. It showed his fatigue and debility after the long journey. He spoke as always, in the most simple words, as a father speaking to his children. He encouraged fraternal love: "Love one another, be humble of heart, do not be discouraged, even by sins committed in your weakness, because discouragement is a Satanic weapon . . ."

His reception at the Provincial Chapter was less rapturous. The activities of the two Cities of the Immaculate were discussed with a freedom and trenchancy that could not but be bruising to a sensitive spirit. It became clear that the necessary support for the Indian city was not forthcoming and that the project was in danger of being abandoned altogether. On the other hand, there were also those who defended the work of Niepokalanow and drew attention to the spirit of fervour and piety that was so evident in the place.

The Chapter proceeded to elect a new Provincial, Father Anselm Kubit, in place of Father Cornelius Czupryk, who had served two three-year terms in that office. Other appointments followed. Father Florian, who had served three years as superior of Niepokalanow, was appointed for another three years, as was customary. Then the blow fell. A new superior was appointed for Mugenzai no Sono, the outgoing Provincial, Father Cornelius. Maximilian was to return there as an ordinary member of the community with particular responsibility for the editing of the *Kishi.*

It was an unheard-of degradation. While superiors were normally appointed for a three year term, it was the almost invariable custom to extend this for a second term except in cases of notable incompetence or unsuitability. Maximilian had founded Mugenzai no Sono and built it up from nothing to its present flourishing condition. He had left it as its superior and founding father: now he must return in what looked like disgrace, stripped of his office and reduced to the ranks. It was a humiliation not to be borne.

But Maximilian did bear it. He had often preached to others the value of obedience. Now he was called on to practise it himself and he did not fail the test.

Accompanied by Father Cornelius, he left Venice on the 31st of August and travelled back to Japan on the same ship, the *Conte Rosso.* They arrived in Mugenzai no Sono on the 4th of October. Maximilian showed the new superior around the friary and the printing works and explained all the details that need to be explained on such an occasion. Then he settled down to his new life as a simple member of the community, no longer in charge of the place he had founded and obliged to ask permission for even the slightest initiative.

Something of what this entailed can be gathered from the testimony given by Father Cornelius during the beatification process.

> On the Japanese mission, Father Maximilian was pressing for an increase in the number of copies printed of the magazine *Seibo no Kishi* (The Knight of the Immaculate). I knew how much he wanted this and I decided to try his religious obedience and put it to the test. With this end in view, I forbade any increase in the number printed without giving any reason for my prohibition. The Servant of God submitted calmly to this order, showing no sign of displeasure and continuing to treat me with every sign of trust and friendship. Subsequently, of course, I withdrew the order.

It was common enough to test the obedience of novices by asking them to follow seemingly senseless orders without questioning. To apply the same procedure to Maximilian in this situation seems like an act of almost wanton cruelty. But if he felt any resentment — and he would hardly be human if he did not — he showed no sign of it on this or other occasions. Cardinal Paul Marella, who was then Apostolic Delegate in Japan, described how he appeared to him at that time.

> He impressed me as a truly dynamic personality, spiritual, balanced, humble and sincere. His face radiated calm and tranquillity. Trusting in the patronage of the Immaculate, he accepted suggestions and advice cheerfully and with a smile. He passed on his devotion to Mary to his religious and they never let themselves be discouraged, even during the terrible events of the war.

He continued to do what he could to keep the Indian project alive, writing to Poland, writing to Rome, writing to Ernakulam. This was another hard burden to bear, not only because of the lost opportunity but because he felt he was breaking his commitment to the Archbishop. He did not agree with the argument that the Polish Province had no one to spare for the work. "I am convinced," he wrote to the Provincial, "that the Fathers who go on the missions are not a loss to the Province but rather the cause of a renewed commitment to their vocation on the part of our young religious and a means of attracting new candidates who will

be authentic, fervent and devoted to their ideals."
It was all in vain. Nothing was done.

Amid all these disappointments and frustrations, he uttered not a word of bitterness or complaint. In his letters, in his diaries, he says nothing of his own feelings. Some hint of his attitude may perhaps be found in a letter of advice he wrote around this time to a Polish priest who was not seeing eye to eye with his superior.

> In general, in our work we should pay particular attention to two things: 1) to being frank and open and sincere in making known to our superiors all our thoughts about any problem; 2) to being exact and single-minded and loving in carrying out the superiors' decisions whether they respect our convictions or not, indeed without even adverting to the fact. However, if the problem is sufficiently important and we can reasonably presume that a higher superior may be of a different opinion, it is lawful to have recourse to him and even obligatory if the problem is very important . . .
>
> In any event, always preserve complete sincerity and joy. May the Immaculate conquer all obstacles and take possession of us all without limitation. It is in that way that she can act through us.
>
> Please pray for me so that I may let myself be completely conquered by her.

In other letters he wrote during this period there is

an increasing pre-occupation with theological matters, particularly in regard to the place of the Blessed Virgin in the plan of salvation. Up to this, his approach to her had been marked more by piety than by any intellectual rigour. Now, influenced to some extent by the criticism of those who disagreed with him, he began to refine and deepen his thought. Writing to the community in Niepokalanow, he answered those who said that devotion to Mary conflicted with devotion to God.

> My answer to them is that the closer you are to the Immaculate, the more freely and openly you can approach the wounds of the Saviour, the Eucharist, the Sacred Heart of Jesus, God the Father. I don't mean that it is necessary that the Immaculate should be actually before your mind at that given moment, since the essence of union with her doesn't consist in thought or memory or emotion but in the will.
>
> I sometimes get annoyed when I am reading and I find an over-anxiety to emphasise that we put all our trust in the Madonna "after Jesus." Obviously this is true in the strict sense. All the same, the exaggerated care not to omit this phrase, granted that it is meant as a sign of respect towards Jesus, still seems to me to be somewhat offensive towards her.
>
> Let us take an example. When the flat presses proved inadequate, we got the rotary press, and we can now say that we put all our

trust in the rotary press to print the *Knight*
on time. If at the same time we always felt
compelled to add "after the factory which
made it," it would suggest that we felt the
machine could let us down and might need to
be returned to the factory. And this would
imply that the factory had not made the
machine to the required standard, which
would certainly not redound to its honour.

It is very characteristic of him that he should draw
his analogy not from the biblical world of seeds
and loaves and wineskins but from the twentieth
century world of printing technology.

His devotion to Mary Immaculate was fully in
the tradition of the Order of Conventual Franciscans. In the Middle Ages when the doctrine of the
Immaculate Conception was being discussed, the
great Dominican theologian, St. Thomas Aquinas,
argued strongly against it. It was a Franciscan theologian, Duns Scotus, who answered these arguments
and paved the way for the definition of the
doctrine by Pius IX many centuries later.
Maximilian liked to recall the teaching of Scotus
and also the decree of the General Chapter of the
Conventuals in the year 1719 which adopted the
Blessed Virgin Mary under the title of the Immaculate Conception as the principal patron of the
Order.

The most important influence on his spirituality
was not however a Franciscan. It was St Louis
Grignion de Montfort, a French priest who died in

1716. His best-known work, *A Treatise on the True Devotion to the Blessed Virgin*, remained unpublished until the manuscript was accidentally discovered in 1842. De Montfort based his Treatise on the narrative of the Annunciation in St Luke's Gospel, where Mary gives her consent before the Incarnation takes place. "God the Father gave his only begotten Son to the world only through Mary," he wrote. "The Son of God became man for our salvation, but in Mary and by Mary. God the Holy Spirit formed Jesus Christ in Mary: but after having asked her consent by one of the foremost ministers of his court." From this he derived his True Devotion, which essentially consisted in consecrating oneself to the Blessed Virgin with all one's possessions, interior and exterior, and even the value of one's good actions, past, present and to come, in the full confidence that she would use all these things to the greater glory of God, in time and in eternity.

Maximilian's admiration for De Montfort's book was such that he once advised his brother to read a little of it every day. One aspect that particularly interested him was its treatment of the relationship between Mary and the three persons of the Trinity. A letter he wrote in 1935 foreshadowed the direction his thought was to take in the last years of his life.

> It will be necessary to reflect more deeply on our knowledge of the Immaculate. Our knowledge of her relations with God the Father,

with God the Son, with God the Holy Spirit, with all the Holy Trinity, with Jesus Christ, with the angels and with us men, so that our knowledge may become ever more luminous through humble and prayerful study. That is a subject which is inexhaustible.

He also conceived the ambition of getting the Conventual Franciscans to consecrate their entire Order to Mary Immaculate in accordance with the decree of 1719. To this end he wrote indefatigably to the Superior General in Rome and to confrères in several countries, suggesting an act of consecration based closely on De Montfort. His suggestion was adopted in 1936, though the act of consecration used was somewhat different from his.

There were other consolations in these years also, other plans of his that came to fruition. One was the launching of the daily newspaper at Niepokalanow. From Nagasaki he kept in close touch with developments, offering advice on technical and editorial matters and criticising in detail the first experimental edition. At a time when anti-Semitism was growing in Poland as well as in Germany, his remarks on the subject are worth noting. "As regards the Jews, I would be very careful not to do anything that would arouse or strengthen hatred against them among those readers who are already ill-disposed or even frankly hostile towards them." The paper appeared in 1935 under the title *Maly Dziennik* (Little Daily) and he was delighted to hear of its rapid increase in circulation.

He was equally pleased with another new publication from Niepokalanow, *The Young Knight of the
Immaculate,* intended for younger readers.

In Nagasaki too some of his dreams were coming
true. By the end of 1935 there were four printing
machines at work in Mugenzai no Sono turning out
65,000 copies of the *Kishi* every month. The community now numbered two priests, twenty Brothers
(of whom four were Japanese) and three students
for the priesthood (one a Japanese). New buildings
had been added, including a small church. The
minor seminary was nearing completion and was
opened the following April. After the opening, a
photograph was taken of the entire population of
Mugenzai no Sono, gathered around the statue of
the Immaculate. Maximilian is in front, with a
patriarchal beard reaching halfway down his chest.
Behind him on one side are the friars and on the
other the boys of the minor seminary, nineteen or
twenty of them in the neat military style uniforms
favoured by Japanese schoolboys of the period.

Shortly afterwards, on the 23rd of May,
Maximilian left Mugenzai no Sono for the Provincial Chapter of 1936. As the boat drew away from
the land, he had a premonition that he would never
see Japan again and his eyes filled with tears.

# Chapter 10
# Harvest Time

Maximilian's last voyage was through a world troubled by war and the shadow of war. In the East, Japan had already swallowed up Manchuria and was now attacking the northern provinces of China. In the West, German troops had just marched into the Rhineland, the first small step in Hitler's plan to bring all Europe under his domination. The smaller states on Germany's borders, Austria, Czechoslovakia and Poland, feared all too correctly that they were next on his list.

The Provincial Chapter was held in Cracow in mid-July. Father Anselm Kubit was re-elected for a second term as Provincial. When discussion turned to Niepokalanow, now by far the largest community in the Province, the usual doubts and criticisms were voiced. But the tide had turned and the future of Niepokalanow was no longer under threat. When one of the delegates described it quite simply as the glory of the Polish Province, he was expressing the opinion of the majority.

For Maximilian there was admiration and concern. Admiration for the graceful and dignified manner in which he had borne all the disappointments and frustrations and shabby treatment of the last three years. Concern for his obviously run-down state of health, which strongly suggested that he should be re-assigned to a position in Poland, at least for the time being. The superior of Niepokalanow, Father Florian Koziura, had completed six years in that office. Maximilian was elected to replace him.

He returned to Niepokalanow in something like triumph. In the space of nine years, the community had grown from twenty to over five hundred, all of them drawn by the personal magnetism of this one man and all of them looking to him as their founder and patriarch. Even during his six years in Japan his influence had been all-pervading and his opinion constantly sought in every new enterprise. Now that he was back there were no limits to the heights that they could scale. They meant no disparagement to the work done by his predecessor. He was a good man, they said, but he wasn't Father Maximilian.

The first thing he did was take three weeks' rest in Zakopane on doctor's orders. Then he returned to Niepokalanow and swung into action. The next three years were to be the happiest of his life. Away from the unfamiliar food and climate of Japan and fortified by an annual holiday in Zakopane, his health improved noticeably. Even more important than the changed physical conditions was the change in the spiritual and emotional level. All his life he had been struggling against obstacles and opposition. Now for the first time he was surrounded by love and respect and enthusiasm and he found within himself resources of strength and energy that had never been tapped before.

Day and night the place literally hummed with activity, for the thunder of the giant rotary presses continued all through the hours of darkness to print the morning editions of the newspaper. The Thirties were the age of the great press lords, men who built vast empires of power and influence through their control of the printed word. Men like William Randolph Hearst in America and Max Beaverbrook in England were renowned for the power they wielded and the flamboyance with which they wielded it and are still remembered today in their fictional counterparts, Orson Welles's Citizen Kane and Evelyn Waugh's Lord Copper. In all this extravagant company there was no stranger figure than the little consumptive friar who in three years became the leading magnate in the Polish media and given a few more years would have taken on the world.

His mind crackled with ideas on every subject, all the way from theology to mechanical engineering. His versatility was astonishing. He would turn from the book he was dictating on the Immaculate to examine the plans for a projected airstrip. One of his Brothers invented an addressograph machine. Two more were sent by him on a course in aviation with a view to starting an aerial delivery service for the newspaper. He was interested in the possibilities of cinema and broadcasting and just before the war started transmitting on his own radio station SP3RN.

By 1939 the community at Niepokalanow

numbered close to eight hundred. The principal edition of *The Knight of the Immaculate* was printing 750,000 copies a month. Two other editions, *The Young Knight* for teenagers and *The Little Knight* for children brought the monthly total to almost a million. There was also the Japanese edition *Mugenzai no Seibo no Kishi* printed in Nagasaki, the Italian edition *Il Cavaliere dell' Immacolata* printed in Padua and a Spanish edition about to be launched in Barcelona. The *Little Daily* was publishing eleven editions a day with a circulation of 137,000 on weekdays and 225,000 on Sundays. Other periodicals coming from Niepokalanow included the *Missionary Bulletin* to encourage interest in the foreign missions, the *Militia of the Immaculate Newsletter* for M.I. groups and study circles, and the *Miles Immaculatae*, a quarterly written in Latin for worldwide circulation to the clergy.

In addition there was his work for the Militia of the Immaculate which now had over a million names on its rolls. He was still pursuing the idea of a foundation in India and was also renewing his interest in Shanghai. Nearer home, a benefactress in Lithuania offered him a site for a City of the Immaculate in Lithuania and he accepted the offer. Plans for this and for many other projects were doomed to be frustrated by the outbreak of the Second World War.

All this activity was achieved without sacrificing any of the tranquillity and prayerful atmosphere of a religious house. There are many independent testimonies to the spirit of unity and brotherhood and common purpose that pervaded the whole place. Father John Burdyszek describes his memories of daily life there in these words:

> The day's work was broken by the usual meals, as a rule lasting no longer than half an hour. The spirit of silence and prayer reigned all day. A visitor might wonder where the large numbers which gathered in the refectory to renew their energy disappeared to so quickly. They would be found in groups at the machines pausing for a moment of recollection before setting these steel giants in motion. There would be a short prayer led by the Brother responsible for each group. Then the machines, named according to years of service "grandmothers," "fathers," "mothers," "children," would begin work. They showed great happiness during their work and they would constantly turn towards the statue of Our Blessed Lady. They lived with the name of Mary. It was like a deep breath refreshing their work with the supernatural intention of doing everything for the love of God.
>
> While the machines were working at full speed a bell would summon them to stop for a short period of adoration before the Blessed Sacrament. The next bell would call all to lunch, and thus would end the first half-day of their daily life. The second half was similar except that the spiritual exercises varied on

different days of the week, as for instance on
Fridays, when all went to the chapel for the
special community commemoration of the
Passion. In the afternoon after recreation
there were instructions and conferences on
religious subjects. On fine days a visitor would
see the large number of religious sitting around
the statue of Our Lady in the gardens listening
attentively to the words of the Father, and he
would notice the strict religious observance of
the Rule, with its spiritual exercises, prayers,
meditations, conferences and adoration of the
Blessed Sacrament.

To all the community Maximilian was "The
Father," In the forenoon he was available in his
little room to anyone who wanted to see him.
There was often a queue outside the door of
Brothers who wanted to discuss problems connected with their work or vocation or spiritual life.
Every Saturday morning he spoke to them in the
chapel, usually on some aspect of Mariology, the
part of theology which deals with the Blessed
Virgin Mary. He also spoke to them in smaller
groups, in the novitiate, in the seminary, in the
refectory, in the infirmary, in the gardens, in the
woods, in a way that was not easily forgotten.

One such talk left an indelible impression on the
Brothers that heard it. One of them afterwards
wrote down a full account of the incident in words
that are strikingly reminiscent of the discourse
after the Last Supper in St John's Gospel. It hap-

pened in the refectory on a Sunday evening in January 1937. After the meal, Maximilian announced the performance of the Christmas play which was about to start in the nearby recreation hall. Then he added unexpectedly that any professed Brother who would prefer to stay on in the refectory and talk with him was welcome to do so.

Most of the community went to the play but a number stayed. He asked them to sit around the table with him in order of seniority. Then he addressed them.

"My dear children, here I am with you. You love me and I love you. I will die and you will remain. Before I go from this world, I want to leave you something to remember me by.

"I wanted to do the will of the Immaculate so I asked those professed Brothers who wanted to stay behind to do so of their own free will. This shows that it was the Immaculate who chose who would be here.

"You call me Father Guardian and that is what I am. You call me Father Director and rightly so, for that is my position in the monastery and in the printing works. But what else am I? I am your father. I am your father more truly than the fleshly father who gave you earthly life. It is through me you received that spiritual life which is divine life and that religious vocation which transcends earthly life. Isn't it true what I am saying?"

Several of the Brothers answered him by acknowledging that they owed their vocation to him and to his publications. Then silence fell as they waited for him to speak again.

He paused for a long time, as if there was something he wanted to say yet found it hard to put into words. He seemed to be labouring under considerable emotion. The air was tense with expectation. Then he resumed.

> "Oh my children, if you knew how happy I am. My heart is full of happiness and peace. The greatest happiness and peace that can be known in this world. In spite of all the troubles of life, there is an indescribable calm in the depths of my heart. My dear children, love the Immaculate! Love her and she will make you happy, trust in her without any limits. It isn't granted to everyone to understand the Immaculate. This can only come as a result of prayer.
>
> "The Mother of God is the most holy of mothers. We know what mother means. But she is the Mother of God and it is only the Holy Spirit who can give the grace of knowing his Spouse whenever and to whomever he chooses.
>
> "I wanted to say something else but perhaps that is enough?"

He looked around at us all somewhat timidly but we urged him to tell us everything and hold nothing back.

"Well, then, I will tell you," he went on. "I've told you that I am happy and full of joy and the reason is that Heaven has been promised to me with complete certainty. My dear children, love Our Lady, love her as much as you can."

He said this with such emotion that his eyes were glistening with tears. There was another moment of silence before he spoke again and said: "Isn't it enough for you to know that much?"

"Tell us more, Father, tell us more. We will never have another last supper like this."

"Since you insist so much, I will say this: what I told you happened in Japan. There, I'll say no more, my dear children, don't ask me any more questions."

Some of those present asked him to go on and give us more details, but in vain: he would say nothing more about these secrets. When we had finished trying to persuade him, he went on in a fatherly way:

"I have told you my secret because I want to give you strength and spiritual courage amid the hardships of this life. There will be difficulties and trials, temptations and spiritual desolations. When these things happen, remember what I said and it will give you a renewal of strength to persevere in the religious life and courage to undertake the sacrifices the Immaculate will ask of you."

Then he asked those present to promise not to repeat anything he had said as long as he was alive. They gave him their word and after another short silence they all left the refectory.

The account of this incident is both attractive and convincing. Maximilian was an intensely private person. In all his letters and articles and talks there is nothing about his own interior life, about his personal prayer and experience of God. The hesitation and even pain that he shows here as he lifts the veil however slightly are entirely in character. Yet something did happen to him in Japan and it can only have been a mystical experience of some kind. It gave him an assurance of salvation that filled him with peace and joy at the very deepest level of his being, where no fear or suffering could touch him any more. The surface might be torn by storms but in the depths there was the stillness that comes from total oneness with the divine.

It was not easy for him to speak of these things to others, even those closest to him. Yet he felt that he was being asked to do so, that the message was not for him alone. So, shyly and yet joyfully, he tried to give them a word of comfort and hope and final victory. He and they would have need of it in the years that lay ahead.

# Chapter 11
# Internment and Release

At dawn on the 1st of September 1939 the German army crossed the border into Poland. Hitler had added Austria and Czechoslovakia to his empire without firing a shot. In Poland he had to fight but the resistance of the Polish army lasted less than a month. After hostilities had ceased, the country was once again partitioned. The western part was taken by Germany, the eastern part by Russia, and the central section was turned into a German puppet-state under a Governor-General appointed by Hitler. This central section, the so-called Government-General of Poland, included Warsaw, Cracow and Niepokalanow.

During the first days of the war the roads leading past the monastery to Warsaw were clogged by retreating military units and streams of refugees. The friars fed and sheltered them to the best of their ability and provided medical treatment for soldiers and civilians injured in the bombing. A number of the more serious cases were given beds in the infirmary and nursed by the Brothers.

The printing of the *Little Daily* was suspended on the 3rd of September. A few days later the first bombs fell on the monastery, causing some damage but no casualties. The Polish authorities ordered the evacuation of the district. Maximilian, who had just been re-appointed superior for a second term by the 1939 Chapter, told the Brothers and seminarians to return to their homes and recommended that they join their local Red Cross. He himself remained in Niepokalanow, together with another priest and thirty-six Brothers, to care for the wounded and to maintain a presence in the monastery.

The first German soldiers arrived on the 12th. They used the monastery grounds as an assembly point for their vehicles but otherwise did nothing to interfere with the life of the friars. Then on the morning of the 19th the community were ordered to assemble and were told by the Germans that they were to be deported to an unknown destination. Two could stay behind to look after the sick: the rest must go at once. Maximilian was urged by the Brothers to stay in Niepokalanow but he felt that his duty was to the community rather than to the place. He named the two who were to remain and was marched off with the others and put on board the trucks that were to take them on the first stage of their journey.

After three days of travel by truck and train they arrived at Lamsdorf in Germany. Two days later they were transferred to the internment camp at Amtitz which was to be their home for the next seven weeks. One of the group, Brother Juventine Mlodozeniec, describes the place in his book *I Knew Blessed Maximilian*.

This camp, with a total capacity for over

12,000 people, consisted of canvas tents arranged in rows, grouped in special regions
separated by barbed wire fencing, reached
only through special gates locked at night. A
street passed through the center of the camp.
Double fencing of barbed wire ran around it.
Sentries, armed with machine guns and
stationed in regularly spaced watchtowers,
were on constant guard.

On the spot they divided us into groups of
200 persons each, destined for different tents.
In each tent were found two benches, a table
made of plain boards and some straw in two
rows on the ground. Posters representing ruins
of Polish cities and villages and bearing inscrip-
tions "England, this is your work" were hung
around the walls. The Germans wanted to
convince us that what befell Poland was not
their fault but that of England.

No one seemed to know why the friars had been
arrested. No charges were ever brought against
them. The camp was run by German army personnel who were on the whole decent men carrying
out orders from higher up. The prisoners were not
treated with deliberate cruelty. The very real hardships they suffered — lack of food, heat, clothing,
beds, shelter, washing facilities — were due to
indifference and inefficiency rather than active ill-
will.

Maximilian immediately set about turning
Amtitz into another City of the Immaculate. He

said to the friars, "If we had wanted to come from Niepokalanow to this concentration camp in order to do apostolic work, who knows how many documents we would need, and we might never have got permission. So let us make the most of this grace that the Immaculate had granted us." He led the way by his example, caring for the other prisoners, visiting the sick, comforting the sorrowful, sharing his sparse rations with the hungry.

The tent became a monastery. One of the Brothers made a statue of the Immaculate from clay and set it up in a prominent place. It was impossible to have Mass and Holy Communion but the Rosary was recited every day before the statue and traditional hymns were sung. The practice of saying the Rosary in common soon spread to the other tents as well.

Around the beginning of November, the friars were told they would soon be released. The officer who was in charge of their region of the camp and who had treated them kindly, asked to have his photograph taken with them. He and Maximilian are in the center on either side of a Brother who is holding the home-made statue. For the first time in ten years, Maximilian is without his beard, which he may have been required to shave off by the camp regulations. After his release he did not grow it again.

They left Amtitz by train on the 9th of November. To their intense disappointment, they only got as far as the Polish town of Ostrzeszow. They were taken to the local secondary school which had been turned into another internment camp and assigned to a room in the basement. Conditions were better than at Amtitz since they now had a roof over their heads. Moreover the local people, many of them readers of the *Knight,* got to hear of their presence and succeeded in sending in fresh bread and other supplies. The commandant of the camp, Lieutenant Hans Mulzer, who had been a Protestant minister in civilian life, proved sympathetic. He wrote afterwards:

> I tried to ease the stay of the religious in the camp as well as I could under the circumstances. I realised that life there was difficult. The imprisonment itself must have been very depressing. They had to sleep on the floor without blankets. The meals were insufficient and the forced inactivity was very wearisome. Above all, they felt keenly the lack of spiritual comfort, being deprived of Holy Mass and Holy Communion for weeks. Nevertheless Father Maximilian Kolbe, with whom I had most contact, as well as his Brothers, never complained to me. On the contrary, they bore their lot with patience and submission until the very hour of their return home. To all this I can attest with a clear conscience and full knowledge.

At the end of the month, they started their traditional novena for the Feast of the Immaculate Conception. On the 7th of December, the eve of the Feast, the commandant brought the news they had all been waiting for: he had been empowered to release them the following day. At Maximilian's request, he arranged for the local priest to bring them Holy Communion on the morning of the Feast itself. Then in a touching farewell ceremony, the two men exchanged simple gifts. The Commandant gave Maximilian a half pound of butter and Maximilian gave him a miraculous medal. The medal was to accompany him safely through the Russian and French campaigns until it was destroyed along with the rest of his belongings in an air raid.

They left Ostrzeszow that afternoon and arrived in Warsaw the following morning. They got back to Niepokalanow the same day with the exception of Maximilian, who stayed on for consultations with the Provincial. He joined the others in the monastery on the 10th of December. Their imprisonment had lasted 82 days.

A period of some fourteen months was to elapse between Maximilian's return to Niepokalanow and his second and final arrest. It was a strange twilight period, an uneasy and uncertain time, lived from day to day and from minute to minute. Peace of a kind came to the defeated and dismembered country and the bulk of the German army moved to the West to attack the British and French forces. Their going brought no relief to the Polish people but rather the reverse, since they were replaced by the S.S. Arbitrary arrests, deportations and executions became part of daily life.

The returning friars found the monastery pillaged but inhabitable. Some of the printing presses had been taken away and the others had been sealed to prevent their being used. Clothing and foodstuffs had been looted. Building materials assembled for the new monastery church were being hauled away. Religious pictures had been torn down and, saddest of all, the statue of the Madonna which had stood there from the very first day had been demolished.

They began at once to repair the damage. Somewhere in the monastery they found an undamaged statue and they set it up again on the traditional spot. They repaired the chapel and were at work on the rest of the buildings when they received word that the Germans were about to billet 3,500 refugees on the place.

Somehow or other they coped. They managed to house and feed them and keep them warm. The refugees had been driven out of Western Poland, the part that had been absorbed by Germany, and ordered to settle in the Government-General. They arrived at Niepokalanow totally destitute, stripped of all their belongings except what they carried in their hands. By dint of extraordinary exertions, the friars provided them with the basic necessities of life. For Christmas, in addition to the usual carols and midnight Mass they arranged a special treat for the children and gave each one a little bag of sweets or cake. For the New Year, they had a similar party for the Jews, who numbered about

1,500 of the 3,500.

As time went on, the German authorities organised food supplies for the refugees and eased the pressure on the friars. At the same time, Maximilian started getting in touch with the scattered members of the community and encouraging them to return. Gradually the numbers built up and the life of the monastery became more normal. In spite of all his efforts, he could not get permission to resume publishing, so he set up various forms of light industry in the monastery which would be of service to the people around: carpentry, shoemaking, maintenance and repair of agricultural machinery and bicycles, watch and clock repairing, manufacture of dairy products. He continued to accept patients in the hospital and also operated a health centre for the locality.

During February the refugees were moved out by the Germans, most of them to houses in the Warsaw area. Before they left, the leaders of the Jewish group formally thanked Maximilian and the friars for their hospitality and asked to have a Mass celebrated in gratitude for all the kindness they had met at Niepokalanow. They promised that if they survived the war they would repay the friars a hundredfold.

A further contingent of refugees arrived in April, about 1,500 in number, none of them Jews. They stayed until July and Maximilian organised First Communion for their children in the month of June.

At the end of July, with most of the refugees

gone and under orders from the Provincial, Maximilian took his annual three weeks' holiday. This time he did not travel far. The monastery had a small rest-house in the nearby woods and it was here that he spent his vacation. Incapable of idleness, he used the time to work on a book about the Immaculate which he had been planning for a long time and for which he had already made some drafts.

During these three weeks he dictated his thoughts to Brother Arnold Wedrowski, who frequently acted as his secretary. The Brother's notes have been preserved and they represent Maximilian's most extended and systematic treatment of the subject. They do not form a connected whole: they are condensed and sometimes cryptic sketches which would have to be expanded and linked by explanatory passages before they could form a book. This Maximilian never lived to do.

The basic theme is summed up in the words which Bernadette heard the Lady say at Lourdes: "I am the Immaculate Conception." The Parish Priest of Lourdes challenged Bernadette on this point. How could the Lady say, "I am the Immaculate Conception"? She could only say, "I am the Immaculately Conceived." A person cannot be a conception, but only the fruit or result of a conception.

Maximilian explained this by saying that a human person cannot be a conception but a Divine Person can. In classical theology the Holy Spirit is described as the fruit of the love between the Father

and the Son; therefore, said Maximilian, the Holy
Spirit is the primal and uncreated conception, all-
holy and all-perfect. The Holy Spirit is the Person
to whom the term Immaculate Conception properly
and primarily applies. So when the Lady at Lourdes
said, "I am the Immaculate Conception" she meant
something more than that she had been conceived
without sin: she meant that she was the Spouse of
the Holy Spirit, so completely one with him and
filled by him that she could take his title as her
own.

The Son, the Second Person of the Trinity,
became flesh in Jesus Christ. Maximilian's thesis
was that the Holy Spirit, the Third Person of the
Trinity, became flesh in Mary, though not in the
same manner. He wrote:

> In her the Holy Spirit miraculously fashioned
> the body of Jesus and made her soul his own
> dwelling place, penetrating her whole being in
> such an indescribable manner that the expres-
> sion "Spouse of the Holy Spirit" is far from
> adequate to express the life of the Spirit in
> her and through her. In Jesus there are two
> natures, divine and human, but one single
> Person who is God; here on the contrary we
> have two natures and two persons, the Holy
> Spirit and the Immaculate, but united in a
> union that defies all human expression.

During the few months of freedom that remained
to him, Maximilian was to return again and again

to this theme. He meditated on it, spoke of it in his talks to the Brothers, wrote or dictated further pages about it whenever the opportunity offered. It was of all subjects the one dearest to his heart.

Ever since his release from the camps, he had been pressing the German authorities for permission to resume publishing *The Knight of the Immaculate.* At this period German policy in Poland was still in a somewhat confused state. There was constant feuding between the civil authority, represented by Governor-General Hans Frank in Cracow, and the security forces, represented by the Gestapo and S.S. in Warsaw. The Governor-General's office gave permission for the publication of the *Knight* but the Gestapo refused to let Maximilian print it. It was not until November 1940 that all the obstacles were removed and the work could go ahead.

The permission given was for one issue of the magazine. It was limited to 120,000 copies and these were to be circulated in the Warsaw district only. It appeared on the 8th of December, the Feast of the Immaculate Conception, and was distributed largely by hand. It avoided political matters and offered a message of spiritual help and comfort which was greatly needed in those troubled times. It bore the date December 1940 — January 1941 as Maximilian hoped that by February he would have obtained permission to resume monthly publication.

In mid-December he visited Cracow for a couple of days, possibly in connection with the question

of the *Knight*. This must have been the last time he
met his mother, who was still living with the
Felician Sisters. No doubt they talked again about
Francis, whose name had kept cropping up in all
their letters. He had deserted his wife and child
some time ago and gone to live with another
woman. His end was to be as unhappy as his life.
He was arrested by the Germans and sent to
Buchenwald where he is believed to have died in
1943. Marianna Kolbe survived the war and died in
1946 at the age of seventy-six.

# Chapter 12
# Prisoner of the Gestapo

The second and final arrest of Maximilian took place at Niepokalanow on the 17th of February, 1941. There has been much speculation about the reasons for his arrest. It has been said that he incurred the hostility of a local collaborator, who denounced him to the Gestapo. It has been suggested that articles criticising Nazi ideals and actions in the *Little Daily* were remembered and held against him. These may have been contributory factors, but the main reason was undoubtedly a much simpler one. He was the kind of man the Nazis did not want in Poland.

The Nazi policy in Poland was now becoming clearer and harder. The main lines had been laid down by Hitler in October 1940 at a dinner party in the Reich Chancellery in Berlin. His guests included Hans Frank, the Governor-General of Poland. As usual on these occasions, Hitler launched into an interminable monologue, this time on the subject of Poland and its place in the new order. His faithful shadow, Martin Bormann, was present and took detailed notes of everything his master said.

Hitler began by spelling out his general plan for Poland. In accordance with his general theory that the Slav races were immeasurably inferior to the German and were indeed barely human, he announced that the future destiny of the Poles was to form a source of unskilled labour at the service of the master race. The Polish peasantry should be allowed to till the soil and produce food for the Germans but the Polish landowners must all be exterminated and so must the educated classes. It might sound cruel, he said, but that was the law of life:

> The Poles will also benefit from this, as we look after their health and see to it that they do not starve, but they must never be raised to a higher level, for then they will become anarchists and Communists. It will be proper therefore for the Poles to remain Roman Catholics: Polish priests will receive food from us and will, for that very reason, direct their little flocks along the path we favor . . . If any priest acts differently, we shall make short work of him. The task of the priest is to keep the Poles quiet, stupid and dull-witted.

Hitler's words were to be the death sentence for all that was best in Polish life. All the natural leaders of the Polish people, priests, writers, artists, university professors, anyone who was in a position to influence the minds and hearts of the nation and who was not prepared to use that influence on the side of the oppressors was marked down for extermination. Among the priests alone, more than three thousand were to die in concentration camps. As a leader and moulder of Polish opinion, Maximilian was doomed.

One avenue of escape was offered him. Any Pole of German descent was allowed to register as a *Volksdeutscher* or ethnic German, and obtain special privileges. According to one witness at the beatification process, Maximilian was approached by a representative of the district authority of Sochaczew, where Niepokalanow was situated, and invited on the strength of his German surname to register as an ethnic German. He was told that this would be welcomed by the German authorities. Obviously they hoped that by doing this he would place his vast moral influence on the side of the occupying forces. He refused the invitation, saying that he was a son of Poland and would always remain so.

Instead of lying low or going into hiding, Maximilian continued to seek permission to publish the *Knight* and wrote twice to the Board of Education and Propaganda in Cracow during January 1941. On the 30th of January he received a formal written refusal and was told not to make any more requests until further notice. By this time, the decision to arrest him may already have been made.

Whether it was this letter or some communication from Warsaw or whether saints have sources of knowledge unknown to the rest of us, Maximilian seemed to know that his time at Niepokalanow was at an end. The first part of February contained two of his favorite Feast days — the Purification of the Blessed Virgin Mary on the 2nd, Our Lady of Lourdes on the 11th — and on these and the other days he gave a series of talks to the community which became known afterwards as the Marian Evenings. He told them of the possibility that he might have to leave them and he reminded them of all he had taught them over the years.

> Our purpose is to increase love for the Immaculate and to inflame the whole world with love for her. For that purpose we work and suffer; for that purpose we want to continue working even after death. That is the most important thing.
>
> I am going away. The purpose of Niepokalanow is not our publishing or any other of our works: they are only means. The purpose is to love the Immaculate.

He spoke very simply and gently but with an urgency and intensity that touched all their hearts. They wrote down all they could remember of his words, to preserve what they knew was meant to be his legacy to them, his spiritual testament.

Early on the morning of the 17th of February Maximilian received word from Warsaw that some German officials were to visit the monastery that day. He used his last hours of freedom to add a few more pages to his book on the Immaculate. Once again he chose his favorite theme, the relationship between Mary and the Holy Spirit. He ended with these words:

> In the Holy Spirit's union with Mary we observe more than the love of two beings: for in one there is all the love of the Blessed Trinity, in the other all of creation's love. So it is that in this union heaven and earth are joined, all of heaven with all of earth, the totality of eternal love with the totality of created love. It is the summit of love.
>
> At Lourdes the Immaculate did not say of herself that she had been conceived immaculate. She said, according to St Bernadette: "Que soy era immaculada conccpciou," I am the Immaculate Conception.
>
> Among human beings the wife takes the name of her husband because she belongs to him, is one with him, becomes equal to him and is with him the source of new life. With how much greater reason then should the name of the Holy Spirit, who is the divine Immaculate Conception, be used as the name of her in whom he lives as uncreated Love, the principle of life in the whole supernatural order of grace.

At 9 a.m. he had a telephone call from the Brother at the gate to say that two cars with Gestapo markings had just driven in. Another Brother who was with him in his room at the time noticed a tremor in his voice as he answered the phone but he soon recovered. "Very good, my son," he said and then added the single word "Maria!"

He left his room and went out to meet his visitors. There were five of them, four in uniform and one in plain clothes. Brushing aside his greeting, they pushed their way into the living quarters of the friars and ordered everyone to leave and to stand in the open space in front of the building. Then they searched through the rooms, apparently in search of some kind of incriminating evidence. They found none but it made no difference. They had been sent to arrest all the priests there and evidence was irrelevant.

At that time the number in the community had built up again to about four hundred and fifty, including seven priests. Two of the priests were lucky enough to escape the net. Towards midday the other five were told that they were under arrest. The Brothers stood there watching silently as the five were led to the waiting cars. One of them succeeded in giving Maximilian a little bag containing some bread and butter. Then the doors were slammed and the cars moved off in the direction of Warsaw.

The Brothers kept his room exactly as he had left it. The visitor today can still see it as it was on that day. In the corner is his simple bed, in the center his wooden chair and writing table. Above the table there is a row of pigeonholes for documents and a statue of the Immaculate. On the table stands his alarm-clock, the hands stopped at ten to twelve, the time he left Niepokalanow for ever.

The five were taken to the Pawiak prison in Warsaw. Little is known of what happened to Maximilian in the next three months. The Pawiak was an old-style prison with small cells and prisoners had little association with one another, apart from their own cellmates.

The Pawiak prison was used by the Gestapo as a reception and interrogation center for newly arrested prisoners. After any information they had to give had been extracted from them, if necessary by torture, they were sent to a concentration camp. It is unlikely that Maximilian and his companions were interrogated at any length as they were not suspected of any anti-German activity. The other four were sent off at the beginning of April to Auschwitz, where two of them were to die before the year was out. Maximilian was kept until the end of May.

He was allowed to write a few notes to Niepokalanow. He had to write them in German so that they could be read by the censor and he had to sign his name as Raymond Kolbe: with typical small-mindedness the Gestapo refused to let him use his religious name of Maximilian. The letters are routine requests for such things as clothes and toothbrushes and food-parcels. They tell little about himself except that his spirit remained unquenched. The letter to Brother Arnold Wedrowski dated the 13th of March is typical of them all.

My dear son,
I got your card of the 3rd of March 1941,

also for the second time parcels of linen. I would ask you not to send me any stationery.

Please do not send me any more parcels unless I specifically ask you.

Look after your health.

Let all the Brothers pray long and well, let them work hard and let them not be downhearted, because nothing can happen without the good God and the Immaculate Virgin knowing it and allowing it.

Heartfelt good wishes to all the Brothers and to yourself.

Raymond Kolbe.

Notwithstanding his words, the Brothers were down-hearted and desperately worried about him and the other priests. Twenty of them drew up and signed a letter to the Chief of Police in Warsaw, offering themselves as prisoners in place of the five priests. Their offer was ignored.

Maximilian was moved around a number of times during his stay in the Pawiak. Few of his cell-mates survived the war but one who did live to tell his story was a man called Edward Gniadek. At the beginning of March, Gniadek was put into cell 103 with a Jew named Singer. He found this a great trial because, as he not very engagingly admitted, he was anti-semitic himself. A few days later they were joined by Maximilian, who at once brought calm to the troubled atmosphere. Soon afterwards Maximilian was to have his first taste of S.S. brutality.

Five days after his transfer to our cell, we had an inspection by the Scharführer, a Nazi. When he saw Father Kolbe in his religious habit I thought he was going to hit him. This man hated not only the religious habit but also and especially the crucifix and rosary which hung from our Franciscan's girdle.

After the Jew gave his report as the senior occupant of the cell, the Scharführer reached for Father Kolbe's crucifix and pulled it roughly, saying, "Do you believe in this?" Father Kolbe answered very calmly, "Yes, I believe."

The German turned purple with rage. Straightaway he hit Father Kolbe in the face. He asked the same question three times, three times he received the same answer and three times he struck him in the face.

I felt like attacking him but I knew it would only make things worse so I tried to hide my anger, since otherwise the guard would have mistreated Father Kolbe all the more as well as taking his revenge on us. Father Kolbe himself, in spite of everything, remained perfectly calm. The only sign of what had happened was the mark of the blows on his face.

After the Nazi left the cell, Maximilian's two companions were considerably more upset than he was. He had to console and calm them rather than the other way round. Shortly afterwards a friendly

Polish guard brought him a prison uniform to wear in place of the habit in order to prevent the same thing happening again. The guard meant well but it is not hard to imagine Maximilian's sadness at parting from the habit he loved so well. Apart from his train journeys in Russia, he had worn the habit of St. Francis for more than thirty years. Even in the internment camps of Amtitz and Ostrzeszow he had been allowed to keep it.

As a result of this beating Maximilian was taken to the prison hospital for treatment. There it was discovered that he was suffering from pneumonia and he was kept for several weeks. At the end of April he was discharged and given a job in the prison library. He continued to get the extra food ration allowed to those on the sick list.

There were still a number of Poles working in the prison service at various levels and these seem to have been doing what they could to save him from the concentration camp and to ease his lot in the Pawiak. His six weeks in the hospital and his transfer to the library were probably due to their efforts on his behalf. But eventually they ran out of delaying tactics. On the 28th of May a consignment of 305 prisoners was sent from Warsaw to Auschwitz and he was among them.

A Pallottine Brother who was in the same consignment described how they were brought to the station and herded roughly into cattle trucks by the guards, who then slammed the doors and bolted them from the outside. In the darkness of the truck there was a moment of deathly silence. Then someone started to sing and gradually the others joined in. He asked someone who the singer was. It was Maximilian.

# Chapter 13
# Auschwitz

The concentration camp at Auschwitz or Oswiecim was planned shortly after the German occupation of Poland. It was built on the model of the camps already being run in Germany by Himmler's terrorist army, the S.S., and it was meant at first to be a detention center for Polish political prisoners. Later on it was to become an extermination center as well and it is estimated that four million people, mainly Jews, died in its gas-chambers between 1942 and 1944. These gas-chambers were only at the planning stage during Maximilian's time there and did not go into operation until some months after his death.

The train arrived at Auschwitz on the evening of the 28th. The prisoners were marched to the camp, a distance of about a mile. Escorted by S.S. men and guard dogs, they passed the outer defences, the watchtowers with their machine-guns and searchlights, the electrified wire fence that meant death to anyone who touched it. Then they went through the entrance gate with its motto *Arbeit Macht Frei* and its carefully tended flowerbed. Finally they were brought to a halt in the parade ground where they were told what lay in store for them. The words used on these occasions were burnt into the minds of all those who heard them.

> You haven't come here to a rest home. You
> have come to a Nazi concentration camp. The
> only way out is through the chimneys. If that
> doesn't suit you, you can always throw your-
> self on to the wire fence.
> If there are any Jews among you, they
> won't live any longer than two weeks. Priests
> can live one month, the rest three months.

As soon as their names had been checked, they
were driven with many blows and curses to the
reception block, a dark and airless hall where they
spent their first night. The following morning they
were marched to Block 26 and made to take off
their clothes. Their heads were shorn and they
were herded into a communal shower room for a
few minutes. They were then issued their prison
clothing. Each man received a uniform consisting
of cap, tunic and trousers made of blue and white
striped material, a shirt, underclothes and a pair of
wooden clogs. The clothes were usually ill-fitting,
tattered and dirty. On the breast of the tunic was
marked their camp number with a red triangle to
indicate that they were political prisoners. The
number was also tattooed on each one's forearm
by means of a specially designed metal stamp.
Maximilians number was 16670.

After this, the newcomers were once again
assembled in the parade ground to be assigned to
one or other of the various barracks, called blocks,

which made up the camp. The Jews and priests were ordered to fall out, since they were destined for particular ill-treatment. The Jews were assigned to the Punishment Squad, which was in effect a death sentence. The priests, the next lowest category among the prisoners, were assigned to Block 17, the forced labor block.

The hatred of the S.S. for priests may seem surprising, given the fact that many of them came from Catholic homes. The Commandant of Auschwitz, Rudolf Höss, who was executed after the war, wrote his memoirs in prison. He describes an upbringing not unlike Maximilian's. His parents were pious, he was given a traditional Catholic education, he even at one stage felt he had a vocation to be a missionary priest. The only reason he gives for turning against the Church was an incident where he suspected that something he told a priest was passed on to his father.

There were however much deeper reasons for the persecution of the Catholic Church by the Hitler regime, among them the Church's condemnation of Nazi policies in regard to abortion and euthanasia. But the fundamental stumbling block was the fact that the Church represented a separate and higher loyalty and that it claimed to judge the morality of the state's actions. The true Nazi was supposed to obey the Führer's orders without question. The Church said he had the duty to question before he obeyed.

The S.S. embodied the Nazi ideology in its most

extreme form. The whole thrust of S.S. training was to inculcate total obedience to the Führer's orders and to root out any lingering trace of religious feeling. After the war a copy of an S.S. act of faith was found in Auschwitz, dated the 30th of April 1940. It read:

> Prayerbooks are things for women and those who wear skirts. We hate the stink of incense. It corrupts the German soul just as the Jew corrupts the German race.
>
> We believe in God but not in his representatives. That would be idolatry and paganism.
>
> We believe in our Führer and in our great Fatherland.
>
> It is for these and these alone that we wish to fight: and when we come to die, it will not be with the words, "Holy Mary, pray for us."
>
> We live like free men and like free men we go from this world.
>
> Let our last breath be: Adolf Hitler!

Jews coming to Auschwitz were promised two weeks of life, priests were promised four. In spite of his health, Maximilian more than doubled the allotted span and survived for eleven weeks in all. The camp records indicate that he arrived on the 28th of May and died on the 14th of August. The only other dates recorded during his time in Auschwitz are two entries in the X-ray register of the camp hospital. These show that he was X-rayed on the 2nd of July and again on the 28th of July.

One other document survives, the last letter Maximilian wrote. It was written to his mother. The letter is brief as it had to be fitted on to a single lined sheet. It is written in somewhat broken German. Because of the censorship, the letter says little and yet it says volumes.

Auschwitz. 15-VI-1941

My dear Mother,

At the end of May I came with a consignment to the camp at Auschwitz (Oswiecim).

I am keeping well.

Dear Mother, be at peace about me and about my health, because the good God is everywhere and he thinks of everyone and everything with great love.

It would be as well not to write to me until you get another letter from me, as I don't know how long I shall be staying here.

With heartfelt love and kisses.

Kolbe Raymond

However his mother may have understood the last sentence, for Maximilian it can have had only one meaning. Many times in the past he had been threatened with death. This time there was no doubt about it. He was living his last days and he decided to live them to the full.

In studying the life of Maximilian Kolbe, one has the overwhelming impression that these last eleven weeks were lived at a different pace and on a different level from anything that had gone before. It was not that he had ever spared himself in the past — far from it — but there is about this period an urgency, almost a recklessness, that bespeaks a man whose time is running out. There is no longer any need for him to consider his health or conserve his strength: he has to use every moment that is left to him.

He saw the will of God in everything that happened. At Amtitz he had told the Brothers that their internment there was a heaven-sent opportunity to minister to their fellow-internees. Now at Auschwitz he had the opportunity to minister to the most wretched and forsaken of all God's creatures. If he had asked for permission to serve as chaplain there, he would have been refused. But now, without asking, the opening had been given to him and he seized on it with eagerness and even joy.

It was not only the pace of his life that seemed to change but the level also. Like every other man, he was the product of his birth and upbringing. He was Polish and Catholic to the core with all the strength that this gave him but also some of the narrowness. In his attitude to outsiders, for instance Jews or Japanese, there was sometimes a touch of superiority, a hint of condescension, a feeling that he saw them as potential conversion statistics rather than as people to be loved. As he pushed the circulation of his publications to new heights and totted up the rising membership of his Militia, there was the danger that the means could become the end and that the good of the organisation could seem more important than the purpose it was meant to serve.

There is nothing of this left in Auschwitz, nothing narrow, nothing nationalistic, nothing sectarian. He does not cease to be a Polish Catholic priest — quite the reverse — but this is no longer a category that in any way separates him from others. His Polishness anchors him all the more firmly in the human family, his priesthood means total openness to the needs of others.

And not just openness but love. In these last weeks every trace of hardness or abrasiveness has vanished from his character. As a young priest on his way up, his relations with his elders had often been strained and the fault can hardly have been all on one side. Later on as a superior himself, he demanded a high level of obedience and austerity from those under him and must at times have seemed a hard taskmaster, even if he never asked others to do anything he would not do himself. But in Auschwitz there is no need for anything except gentleness and compassion and total self-giving. He grows before our eyes. A good man becomes a saint.

Maximilian of Auschwitz rises above all barriers of race or religion. As he reached to everyone in that place at that time, so he reaches out to everyone today. He is a universal man.

One of his fellow-prisoners, an engineer, summed him up in these words:

From our meetings with him we came away

with our spirits consoled and our wills strengthened to stand fast and not give way. He urged us to trust in God and to put ourselves under the protection of the Immaculate. I heard from my fellow-prisoners how the influence of the Servant of God was being described as a kind of "reign" among the prisoners. That was the effect of his actions and of his blessed influence upon his fellow-prisoners.

There were many opportunities for Maximilian to minister to his fellow-prisoners. In a concentration camp, unlike a prison, all activities were done in common. The prisoners had no privacy. By day or night there was not one moment when they were not under scrutiny from a hundred eyes.

They slept in communal dormitories in the different blocks, on wooden bunks with straw mattresses, sometimes two or even three to a single bunk. In the morning they were lined up in the parade-ground for the roll-call of the day. These roll-calls were meant to ensure that no prisoner was missing and they were often protracted for hours on end, during which time the prisoners had to remain standing at attention. Then they received their breakfast, which consisted of one half-litre of sweetened black coffee or tea and nothing else. After the morning's forced labour, their midday meal was a bowl of watery vegetable soup. There was further work in the afternoon, after which came the evening roll-call. Supper consisted of a half-litre of coffee or tea, 300 grammes of bread and with it either a piece of sausage or margarine or cheese or a spoonful of jam. The calorie content of the food ration was below what is needed by an adult in a state of rest. These men were made to perform manual labour of the heaviest kind. Any prisoner who did not succeed in "organising" (as the camp slang called it) extra rations, inevitably died of starvation if he did not die first of ill-treatment or disease.

Maximilian and the other priests who arrived with him were assigned to work on the building of a wall around the crematorium. Forced labour meant that they were supposed to do everything "at the double", that is, running. If they paused at all, they were liable to be beaten by the guards. Maximilian was told to carry gravel in a wheel-barrow. The barrow was large with a small wheel and he himself was still suffering from the after-effects of pneumonia. Another prisoner took pity on him and wheeled a few loads for him. One of the guards saw this, beat them both, and then forced each of them in turn to wheel the barrow with the other sitting on top of the load of gravel. Maximilian never again let another prisoner risk punishment by helping him.

After a few days of this work he was transferred to an area called Babice, a short distance outside the camp. Here the work consisted of cutting reeds and tying them into bundles to help with the drain-age of the marshy land. The capo in charge of this section was a convicted criminal called Krott who was known for his brutality towards priests. Here again Maximilian was beaten by the guards and savaged by their dogs. One of those who saw him being mistreated and marvelled at his patience was a Polish soldier Francis Gajowniczek, the man who was later to be saved by him from the Death Cell.

During any free periods in the camp Maximilian put himself at the service of anyone who wanted to see him, even though priests were forbidden to exercise their ministry. His fame began to spread throughout the camp. The artist Mieczyslaw Koscielniak tells how he was brought to see him on the Feast of Corpus Christi, the Body of Christ.

> I looked at him attentively and a little curiously but without surprise. We were both scorched with the sun, black with dirt, dressed in rags, stripped you might say of human appearance, of dignity, of freedom. Taking care not to attract the attention of the other prisoners, we walked to where the new block was being built (Block 17) and sat down on the bricks and planks.
>
> Father Kolbe began to talk in a low voice about the Feast of Corpus Christi, about the great and all-powerful God, about the suffering he sends to prepare us for a better life, and he encouraged us to persevere and take heart because the time of trial must pass. "There is a divine justice," he said, "and it will be made manifest to all, so there is no need to lose heart."

We listened spellbound, forgetting for the moment our hunger and degradation. He went on: "No, no, they will never kill our souls. We prisoners are different from those who are persecuting us. We are Catholics and Poles and they cannot kill our dignity. No, we will never give in, we will persevere to the end, none of their terrors will ever kill the Polish soul. And if we die, we will die in holiness and peace, resigned to the will of God."

Thus spoke Father Maximilian Kolbe, Franciscan, great priest, later to be the hero and martyr who gave his life for a fellow-prisoner. Strengthened in spirit, we made our way back to our blocks.

In return Koscielniak made two little drawings, one of Christ and one of the Blessed Virgin, and Maximilian carried them with him everywhere. After the war the artist painted a series of pictures which showed different incidents in Maximilian's last months, from his arrest to his death. They are now in Niepokalanow and have been reproduced around the world.

On everyone he met he made the same impression. "I used to meet him after the evening roll-call," a veterinarian testified, "and his words gave me strength and hope to bear my sufferings, along with a great and deep contentment and joy. He spoke in such a way that after hearing him I felt full of courage and felt no more fear of death, even though it threatened me all the time. He used to gather the prisoners around him, encouraging them and giving them spiritual consolation."

He spoke to them by day and by night, individually and in groups. He urged them to have no hatred for the Germans and he showed none himself, no matter how badly he was treated. Once, after he had been kicked by a guard, a prisoner heard him murmur, "May God forgive you," which was the nearest he ever came to showing impatience. He often ended his talks by hearing the confessions of the prisoners. One priest who came to him for confession was asked by Maximilian to hear his in return. He came away with the conviction that he had met a saint.

He prayed constantly. Prisoners noticed how he made the sign of the cross before eating, even though he risked being beaten for this sign of religion. A man who slept next to him saw how he used to kneel and pray in the Block at night. The same man succeeded in getting some communion breads while working outside the camp and enabled Maximilian to say Mass on two occasions and give Holy Communion to some of the prisoners. At other times, as a symbolic gesture he would bless his meagre bread ration and distribute it among his companions, refusing to accept any of theirs in return.

He gave everything away. He exchanged his clogs with a prisoner who had a worse pair. He took no gifts from others, neither food nor clothing nor money: though he did once accept some medals with gratitude and distribute them among his companions. He refused anything that looked like special treatment. It was hard to persuade him to keep even the little food that formed the official ration. A tailor testified:

> I saw how one time in front of the Block he gave his dinner, about three-quarters of a litre of soup, to a younger prisoner from the Juvenile Block, saying, "Take this and eat it, you are young, you have to live." Another time he tried to do the same thing but we wouldn't let him, we made him eat it himself.

This extreme self-denial, of which we shall meet more examples, seems at first sight foolhardy and even morbid. But there can be no doubt that this course of action was adopted with a purpose. "He never exposed himself thoughtlessly to ill-treatment or blows," the same man testified. "On the contrary, he always acted with full premeditation and with a clear awareness of what he wanted to achieve." Evidently what he wanted to achieve was to witness to the power of love. In a place where survival was the only aim, where prisoners fought over a scrap of bread and killed for a pair of shoes, he deliberately chose to live by a totally different set of values. One extreme must be countered by another. Fire must be fought with fire. Every time he shared his food or gave away his clothing or stood back and let another take his place, he was defying Auschwitz and all that it stood for.

Many other incidents are related of him during

this period, the month of June 1941: writing letters for those who knew no German, making peace between those who quarrelled, washing the mess-tin of a prisoner who had been beaten on the hands, helping another to carry corpses to the crematorium. And it must be remembered that only a tiny fraction of those who were in Auschwitz survived to tell their stories after the war ended in 1945. For every instance of his kindness and compassion that has been recorded there must have been a hundred that are known only to God.

One day around the beginning of July an incident occurred which almost proved fatal. The infamous Krott was in a particularly vicious mood and he kept heaping heavy loads of wood on Maximilian's back and forcing him to run with them. When the victim fell to the ground he kicked and abused him savagely. At the midday break he forced him to lie on a tree trunk and ordered another prisoner to give him fifty lashes. Then, more dead than alive, Maximilian was thrown into a ditch and covered with branches.

When evening came, some of the other prisoners carried him back to the camp and put him to bed. The next day he was still scarcely able to move and he was brought to the camp hospital.

There can be no better illustration of the twisted mentality of the S.S. than the existence of a hospital in Auschwitz. Somewhere back in the early thirties when the first concentration camps were being planned, it must have been laid down that there should be a hospital in every camp. So Auschwitz had a hospital. It made no difference that the whole place was dedicated to the systematic destruction of human life. The regulations said there had to be a hospital so there was a hospital. Prisoners who had been reduced to human wrecks by the machinery of camp life were taken into its overcrowded and under-equipped wards and given primitive treatment. If they recovered they were sent out once more into the camp so that the whole process could begin all over again.

This was not Maximilian's first visit to the hospital. A Polish physician, Dr Rudolf Diem, himself a prisoner, was assigned to work in the hospital and he was later to describe how Maximilian had been sent to him suffering from fever and congestion of the lungs. Dr Diem offered to take him in but Maximilian refused. Instead he pointed to another prisoner, one of the hundreds who came to the hospital each day, and asked that he be taken in his place. Surprised, the doctor asked, "Who are you?" Maximilian answered, "I am a Catholic priest." More than once subsequently the doctor made the same offer to Maximilian and received the same courteous but firm refusal.

This time refusal was impossible since Maximilian was unable even to walk. He was given a bed and X-rayed and the diagnosis was that he was suffering from pneumonia in addition to his other injuries. One of the prisoners who worked as orderlies in the hospital was a young priest, Father Conrad Szweda, and he describes Maximilian's condition at that time. "He was not delirious. His face was covered with bruises, his eyes were glazed and his temperature was so high that his tongue was stiff and rigid and his voice died in his throat."

After some days, the pneumonia passed through its crisis. Maximilian survived but his temperature remained high so he was transferred to the ward reserved for typhus patients and suspects. Here he was given a bed near the door, which made it easier for other patients to come to him. Father Szweda reports:

> Among his sick and suffering brothers, he exercised his ministry as a shepherd of souls. He told them stories drawn from his rich fund of experiences, he heard their confessions, he recited prayers in common with them, he raised their spirits and spoke to them about the Immaculate Virgin, whom he loved with the simplicity of a child. Under cover of darkness, those confined there used to come to him for confession or for words of comfort.
>
> When I came to him after work each day, he would hold me to his heart like a mother embracing her child, he would comfort me and tell me to take the Immaculate as my model, saying, "She is the true consoler of the afflicted, she listens to everyone, she helps everyone." I always came away consoled and at peace.
>
> Once I managed to bring him a cup of tea. I was amazed when he wouldn't take it. "Why

should I be an exception?" he said. "The others don't have any."

Here again Maximilian saw the hand of Providence in his situation. The sick and dying were in need of a priest — and there he was. He put himself completely at their disposal. Day or night, he was never too sick or too tired to listen to their troubles and say a consoling word. One prisoner, a university graduate, relates how he and other patients used to creep along the floor at night to Maximilian's bedside.

> His words were profound and simple. He urged me to believe firmly that good would be victorious.
> "Hatred is not a creative force," he whispered, his fevered hand gripping mine. "These sorrows won't overcome us. They will help us to be stronger. We must suffer them and other sacrifices so that those who remain after us will be happy."

The same witness tells how both he and Maximilian left the hospital on the same day. They were not discharged as cured but were summarily expelled by the capo in charge, an unstable individual whose feelings of inferiority showed themselves chiefly in a hatred of anyone whom he regarded as an intellectual. Maximilian was assigned to the Invalid Block, originally intended to be a convalescent center for those discharged from the hospital. The inmates of the Invalid Block were excused from heavy work but they were only given half rations of food, which did not help their chances of recovery.

It was now nearly the end of July. Maximilian had spent two months in Auschwitz and he was still alive, still moving around, still speaking the word. People who knew him before the war could not recognise him. His famous beard was gone, his head shaved, his face haggard and emaciated, his arms and legs like matchsticks. Only his eyes, burning like coals in their deep sockets, showed that his spirit was unquenched.

After about a week in the Invalid Block he was transferred to Block 14. On the afternoon of the last Sunday in July he spoke to a group of prisoners outside the Block. The subject of his talk was his favorite one, the relationship of the Immaculate to the Persons of the Blessed Trinity. The theme was an abstract one but he spoke with such a burning intensity that his hearers were completely absorbed. For a little while Auschwitz and all its horrors ceased to exist for them. It was the last time they were ever to hear him speak.

# Chapter 14
# The Death Cell

One day during the following week a prisoner from Block 14 escaped. It was not all that difficult for a prisoner to escape if he was working outside the camp. His absence would not be discovered until the evening roll-call.

To discourage such attempts, the S.S. took brutal revenge on those who were left behind. Any prisoner who escaped knew that he was condemning ten of his comrades to an excruciating death from hunger and thirst in the cellars of Block 11, known as the Death Block.

At the roll-call that evening it was discovered that Block 14 was one man short. For three interminable hours the whole camp stood at attention in the parade-ground while the guards checked and counted. Not until nine o'clock were the prisoners allowed to dismiss and receive their miserable evening meal. Those from Block 14 received no meal. Their food was poured down the drain before their eyes and they were sent to their beds to spend the night in terror of what the morrow would bring.

The next day, after the morning roll-call, the other blocks were sent off to work. Block 14 were told to remain standing at attention in their places.

Hour after hour passed and they still stood there, starving, parched, exhausted, terrified. As the sun rose in the sky and beat down on their heads, they began to faint, one after another. When they fell to the ground, they were dragged roughly to one side and piled in an untidy heap.

Around three o'clock in the afternoon the survivors were given a short break and allowed to take some food. Then they were made to return to their places on the parade-ground and await the return of the others from work for the evening roll-call.

After the roll-call was over, Lagerführer Karl Fritzsch approached the prisoners of Block 14 accompanied by officials and guards. The Lagerführer or Camp-Leader was next in rank to the Commandant and was responsible for the day-to-day life of the prisoners, a responsibility which Fritzsch discharged with notable brutality. The Commandant himself in his memoirs was to describe him as "a distasteful person in every respect." A deathly silence fell over the ranks as Fritzsch announced that the fugitive had not been recaptured and that ten men from his Block must die in his place.

The silence continued as Fritzsch walked slowly along the lines, savouring to the full the power of life and death that lay in his hands. With a careless flick of his finger, he indicated first one victim, then another. An officer beside him noted down the numbers as the condemned men left the ranks and stood apart on one side. No sound was to be heard except for a cry of despair from one of the prisoners selected. It was Francis Gajowniczek, lamenting the fact that he would never see his wife and children again.

At that moment something happened that was totally unexpected and totally unprecedented. A prisoner stepped out of the ranks and said something in a low voice to Fritzsch. Few of the prisoners could see or hear exactly what was going on. One who did see and hear was Dr Nicetas Wlodarski. This is how he remembered it later.

> After the ten prisoners had been chosen, Father Maximilian stepped out of the line, took off his cap and stood at attention in front of the Lagerführer. He was taken aback by Father Maximilian and he said, "What does this Polish swine want?"
>
> Father Maximilian pointed towards Francis Gajowniczek, who had already been chosen for death, and answered: "I am a Polish Catholic priest. I am old. I want to take his place, because he has a wife and children."
>
> The Lagerführer was so surprised that he could hardly speak. After a moment he waved his hand and said the one word, "Out!" Then he ordered Gajowniczek to go back to the line which he had left a moment earlier. That was how Father Maximilian took the place of the condemned man.
>
> The distance between me, Fritzsch and Father Maximilian was not more than three metres. A little while later, the ten condemned

men were shut up in Block 11.

What thoughts were in Maximilian's mind during the selection, what motives led him to take the decisive step, will never be known. It may seem idle and impertinent to speculate about them. Yet the event is too important to be passed over without comment. It is crucial not only in the history of this one man but in the whole history of our age. At a time and in a place of unparalleled horror, this stands out as a moment of pure grace. The image of the prisoner confronting his persecutor, the weak confounding the strong, burns itself into the mind. Among all the dreadful images of the twentieth century, this one speaks of goodness and hope.

Our speculation is made easier by the fact that this action of Maximilian's is so much of a piece with the rest of his life, and especially with his life as a prisoner. Time and time again in Auschwitz we see him doing things for others which seem to have a symbolic as well as a practical meaning. When he divides his bread, gives away his meal, exchanges his clogs, refuses a gift of money or a cup of tea, asks that another be taken by the hospital in his place, he is saying something that is louder than words. It is not enough to speak about love in a place where hatred reigns supreme. Love must be acted out as totally and as unreservedly as possible. When everything else has been given, then only life remains. Greater love than this no man has than to lay down his life for his friend. Maximilian's action was the logical culmination of all that had gone before.

There is one other way in which this act completes the pattern of his life. He saw all his trials and troubles, especially those of the last two years, as so many opportunities for doing the will of God. In the discomfort and uncertainty of Amtitz, in the bleak hopelessness of Auschwitz, in the misery and squalor of the camp hospital, he saw people who needed his help and he thanked God that he was there to give it. Now one last opportunity was being offered him. Who were more forlorn and abandoned, who were more in need of his ministry than these wretches on their way to a painful and protracted death? How better spend the little life that remained to him than by sharing and lightening their sufferings?

Thoughts of this kind must certainly have been in his mind as Fritzsch paced along the silent ranks. They had by now become part of the permanent background to all his conscious actions. But the actual moment of decision can hardly have been the result of a logical process. Dazed, parched, exhausted, weakened by hunger and disease, drawing on his last reserves of strength just to remain standing upright, his reactions were more on the level of instinct than of thought. He heard Gajowniczek's cry and responded. His response showed the kind of man he had become.

Block 11 has a sign over the door which says *Blok Smierci*, the Death Block. Its basement contains the cells where prisoners were tortured in different ways. Beside it is a rectangular yard enclosed by high walls, where thousands were executed by firing squads. Prisoners who climbed the six steps to the door of Block 11 were never seen again alive. Others were forbidden even to approach the building.

When the ten men had been led away to the Death Block, they passed for ever beyond the knowledge of the rest of the camp. On the evening of the second day the young priest Conrad Szweda, relying on a certain latitude accorded to hospital personnel, approached one of the guards outside Block 11 and inquired about Maximilian. He received the rough reply, "Do you want to go in there too? Don't you know you're not allowed to ask any questions about them?" That was all the information he could get.

That might be the full extent of our information too were it not for the presence in Block 11 of a Polish prisoner named Bruno Borgowiec. He was employed there as a secretary and translator, since he spoke both German and Polish fluently, and he witnessed the last days of Maximilian and of many others besides. The S.S. did not like to have witnesses of their misdeeds and those who worked in Block 11 rarely survived to tell their stories. But Borgowiec was careful and discreet. He saw nothing and said nothing and survived until the end of the war.

After the war *The Knight of the Immaculate* was revived during Poland's brief period of freedom between the Nazi and Communist tyrannies. Young

Father Szweda wrote an article in it giving his recollections of Maximilian's time in Auschwitz and Borgowiec read it. Like many of the survivors of the concentration camps he was broken in health and knew that he had only a short time to live. He went to the Church authorities and made a sworn statement about Maximilian's time in the Death Cell. He had no trouble in remembering: as he said himself, "the impression of these things will remain for ever engraved upon my memory." He died soon afterwards, in March 1947.

Borgowiec's statement gives a factual and detailed account by an eye-witness of events which otherwise would be known only by rumour and hearsay. The preservation of this witness can only be described as providential. He deserves and indeed demands to be quoted from at length.

He begins by describing Block 11 and his own work there. Then he goes on to tell of the arrival of the ten prisoners.

> After being ordered to undress completely outside the Block, the condemned men were herded inside, where there were already twenty victims of the previous trial. The new arrivals were put into a separate cell. As they were locked in, the guards called out mockingly, "You will wither away like tulips!" From that moment on the poor wretches received no more food.
>
> Every day the guards made an inspection and gave orders for the bodies of those who

died during the night to be taken away. I was always present at these inspections as I had to register the names of the dead and also translate from Polish into German any conversation or requests made by the prisoners.

From their cell each day came the sound of prayers being said out loud, the rosary being recited, hymns being sung. The prisoners in the other cells joined in. Sometimes when the guards were not there I would go down into the basement to talk to them and comfort them. Their fervent prayers and hymns to the Blessed Virgin could be heard all through the basement. I felt as if I was in church. Father Maximilian would lead and all the others would respond. Sometimes they were so deep in prayer that they didn't hear the guards coming for the regular inspection. Only when the guards shouted at them did their voices fall silent.

When the cell-door was opened, the poor wretches would cry out and beg for a piece of bread or a drop of water, which was refused. If one of the stronger ones made for the door, he was at once kicked by the guards in the stomach and fell back dead on the floor or was shot out of hand.

The kind of martyrdom suffered by the prisoners condemned to this dreadful death can be gathered from the fact that the bucket was always empty and dry, which means that the poor wretches were so thirsty they drank their own urine.

Father Maximilian Kolbe of blessed memory bore himself like a hero. He made no requests and no complaints. He gave courage to the others and encouraged them to hope that the fugitive would be found and they would then be released.

As they grew weaker, they said their prayers in a lower voice. During the inspections, when the others were lying on the floor, Father Maximilian could be found standing or kneeling in the middle, looking calmly at whoever was coming in. The guards knew about his act of sacrifice and they knew that all those dying with him were innocent. They were so impressed by him that they said, "That priest is a truly remarkable man. We have never had anyone like him here before."

Two weeks passed in this way. Meanwhile the prisoners had died one by one. Only five remained alive into the third week, among them Father Kolbe. The authorities decided it was going on too long. The cell was needed for other victims.

So one day, the 14th of August, they fetched the director of the infirmary, a German criminal by the name of Bock, and he gave each of them an intravenous injection of poison acid in the left arm. Father Kolbe offered his arm to the executioner with a prayer on his lips. I could not stand the sight any longer so I pretended I had work to do in the office and went away.

When the guards had gone off with the executioner, I went back to the cell. I found Father Maximilian Kolbe sitting with his back to the wall, his eyes open and his head leaning to the left in his customary attitude. His face was serene and beautiful and radiant.

The death certificate issued later by the camp gave the time of his death as 12.50 p.m. on the 14th of August 1941. Borgowiec and another prisoner took his body and placed it in a wooden box. It lay that night in the mortuary cell.

The following day it was taken to the crematorium and burnt. The chimney scattered his ashes to the four winds. It was the 15th of August, the Feast of the Assumption of the Blessed Virgin Mary.

# Chapter 15
# The Meaning of
# Maximilian

More than forty years have passed since the death of Maximilian Kolbe. During these years his fame has steadily grown. After the war, articles about him began to appear in newspapers and magazines, then as interest in him increased full-length biographies followed. Church authorities in Poland, Italy and Japan began to collect the sworn testimony of those who knew him. Devotion to him grew and miracles were attributed to his intercession. His beatification came in 1971 and his canonization in 1982.

When the Church canonizes a man and declares him to be a saint, it is not merely making a statement about his own personal holiness. It is holding him up as an inspiration and an example to others. The canonization of Maximilian Kolbe makes us ask what relevance he had for the world of today, a world which questions so many of the things that he lived and died for.

In Poland today there is no problem about his relevance, but one reason for this lies in the fact that Poland has been isolated from the rest of the world for the last forty years. They have been forty years of more or less continuous persecution for the Church in Poland, sometimes violent, sometimes concealed, but never far away. In time of persecution people draw together, loyalty is paramount, differences are not aired, the line is held.

Polish Catholicism today could fairly be described as conservative. Anything which bears the label "progressive" is suspect, largely because the word has been taken over by the Communist government and its agencies. The Catholic publishing house Pax has issued translations of leading European and American theologians but because Pax is supported by the government loyal Catholics shun them. The pious practices of the past still flourish: processions, pilgrimages, stations of the cross, devotions to the Blessed Virgin. In many ways the Polish Church seems to be still living in the nineteen-thirties.

Into this atmosphere Maximilian Kolbe fits very comfortably. Indeed, he more than any other single man is responsible for its character and its endurance. His publications moulded the spirit of Poland in the thirties, strongly Catholic and strongly nationalist. His courage in the face of persecution kept his memory alive after his death and made him a rallying point for a Church still undergoing many trials. His spirituality, with its emphasis on the intercession of the Immaculate and its reliance on such traditional aids as medals and statues, is still in the mainstream of Polish spirituality.

In the wider world the situation is somewhat different. Even during his lifetime some of his contemporaries felt unease at his constant invocation of the Immaculate. That feeling remains today. It is the balance rather than the orthodoxy of his teaching that is questioned. Since the Second Vatican Council there has been a growing awareness in the Catholic Church that there have been excesses in Marian devotion in the past, and this awareness has been sharpened by the opening of dialogue with Christians of the Reformation Churches. Many of the traditional devotions and practices in honour of the Blessed Virgin have declined in popularity and there has been relatively little recent thinking and writing in the field of Mariology.

The coming of Pope John Paul II has altered this situation. It would not be inaccurate to describe him as a spiritual child of Maximilian Kolbe. Karol Wojtyla grew up in the Poland of the *Knight* and the M.I. He endured the terror of the Nazi occupation and narrowly escaped arrest more than once. As Archbishop of Cracow, he had Auschwitz in his diocese and many times visited and prayed in the death-cell. At the time of Maximilian's beatification in 1971, he described him as a model for priests and a pioneer in Mariology. At a press conference in Rome he said:

He wished to bear witness by his life and death to his love for our Lady, whom he invoked under her title of the Immaculate Conception. His Marian theology possesses a doctrinal accuracy that enchants those familiar with that keystone of Vatican II, *Lumen Gentium*. One is tempted to say that he had foreseen, even in its wording, the admirable eighth chapter consecrated to the Virgin Mary.

The spiritual fecundity of this humble religious, who was not only a marvel of efficiency — something that our technocratic world appreciates — but also one of the greatest contemplatives of our time, bears witness before the entire world to the unique role played by the Virgin Mother of God.

The election of Cardinal Wojtyla to the Papacy has heralded a revival in Marian devotion. He made this clear from the beginning by incorporating the letter M into his papal coat of arms in defiance of all the rules of heraldry. Since then he has spoken on numerous occasions about the Blessed Virgin and made pilgrimages to her shrines in many parts of the old and new world. When he visited Poland in 1979, he returned once again to the death cell in Auschwitz and there, on the spot where Maximilian died, recited the fourth glorious mystery of the rosary, the Assumption of the Blessed Virgin.

In his Marian doctrine, John Paul II has not entered into some of the more rarefied areas of Maximilian's thought. He has concentrated instead on the figure of Mary that is presented to us in the official teaching of the Church. He has invoked her as the sinless Mother of God who is also Mother of humankind and a model of all the qualities that this sinful world so sorely needs. "This is the woman of history and destiny who inspires us today," he said in Washington, "the woman who speaks to us of femininity, human dignity and love, and who is the greatest expression of total consecration to Jesus Christ, in whose name we are gathered today." In the person and teaching of this Pope, Maximilian's love for the Immaculate is reaching and touching a greater audience than even he had ever dreamed of.

John Paul II has also praised Maximilian for his attitude to modern technology and communications. He was not at all frightened of scientific advances: on the contrary, he revelled in them. New techniques in mass communication were welcomed by him as so many more ways of preaching the gospel. He was fascinated by machinery and all things mechanical and he passed on this spirit to his Brothers. They had the same kind of affection for their gigantic printing presses as the mediaeval monks had for their bells: they even gave affectionate nicknames to the various machines. Father Burdyszek recalls the words which Maximilian used in blessing a new electric motor:

> Brother Motor! What ought I to wish him? To print well? To serve our Blessed Queen and Mother faithfully? Today he's blessed and he takes the habit. Next he will be prepared, that will be his novitiate. Then he will be put to work and that will be his profession.
>
> What more shall I wish him? That he may work for a long time? That he may have plenty of companions? That he may be efficient? Ah, no! I wish him but one thing: that he may follow the desires of our Lady. A

good religious is good not because he does much, but because he obeys.

So, Brother Motor, you will be a good religious machine if you do exactly what the Holy Virgin demands of you, whether it be to retire tomorrow or work for a hundred years.

There is an authentic echo here of St Francis, who praised Brother Fire and Sister Water. Many of Maximilian's confrères thought otherwise and we have seen how much opposition he encountered from those who felt that a Franciscan friary should be a place for silence and withdrawal. But he himself believed that the thundering rotary presses were the modern equivalent of the ancient scriptorium, where rows of monks copied out manuscripts and the only sound was the scratch of pen upon parchment. When one scandalized visitor asked him, "What would St. Francis say if he saw all this?" is said to have replied, "He would roll up his sleeves and join in the work." Scientific and technical developments are not temptations to be avoided but opportunities to be grasped. Science is too important to be left to the scientists.

These aspects of his life have their undoubted relevance today but they are not the central reason for his appeal to the modern world. It is because of his death that he was judged worthy of the honor of canonisation and the title of saint. It is because of his death that John Paul II spoke his name in Canterbury Cathedral and lit a candle to his memory. It is because of his death that this book is being written and read.

The usual definition of a martyr is someone who gives his life for the Christian faith or for one of the Christian virtues. The virtue which inspired Maximilian's death was surely the virtue of love, and love in its purest form. In the last days of his life he became a truly prophetic figure, a living embodiment of the virtue of love in the midst of the greatest monument ever erected to the power of human hatred.

A place like Auschwitz had a totally demoralising effect on everyone it touched. This was true not only of the guards but also of the prisoners. Rudolf Höss, the Commandant of Auschwitz, admitted this in his memoirs and gave this harrowing example.

> I once saw, from a window of my house, a Russian dragging a food-bucket behind the block next to the command building and scratching about inside it. Suddenly another Russian came around the corner, hesitated for a moment, and then hurled himself upon the one scrabbling in the bucket and pushed him into the electrified wire before vanishing with the bucket. The guard in the watchtower had also seen this, but was not in a position to fire at the man who had run away. I at once telephoned the duty block leader and had the electric current cut off. I then went myself into the camp to find the man who had done

it. The one who had been thrown against the wire was dead and the other was nowhere to be found. They were no longer human beings. They had become animals, who sought only food.

Under the glare of the searchlights at Auschwitz, the true character of Maximilian was revealed in all its unexpected glory. It was strange enough to hear a prisoner speaking of love and forgiveness. It was more than strange, it was incredible, to hear a prisoner freely offering his life for another. In a place where survival was all that mattered, where a man could kill another for a scrap of food, this action fell like a thunderbolt on guards and prisoners alike. There was no precedent, there was no explanation. It upset all the accepted ideas, it laughed at common sense, it broke the mold of selfishness and self-interest and self-preservation that shaped and contained all their lives. Every day many people died at Auschwitz but this one death was unique.

A great deal is written and spoken today about the theology of liberation, about the duty of the Christian to free his fellow man from political and economic oppression. We are sadly aware that cruelty and injustice are still active in the world, that imprisonment without trial is still frequent and widespread, that torture of prisoners has become routine procedure in many different countries. We know that liberation is needed but we wonder if it will ever come.

We are always fighting the war that is to end war. Every liberation opens the way to a new slavery. Every peace breeds another war. We have been told, by Alexander Solzhenitsyn and others, that the Russians who liberated Auschwitz in 1945 were at the same time building huge concentration camps to hold their own dissidents: in fact, Solzhenitsyn himself was arrested in the course of the campaign which drove the Germans from Poland. We wonder if there is any possibility of real liberation. We wonder if there is any such thing in the world as a free man.

Maximilian Kolbe gives us our answer. He was a free man. He was never more free than when he was most closely confined. There are those who say that freedom of the body must come before freedom of the spirit. They tell us that it is useless to preach the Good News to the poor or to the hungry or to the oppressed: we must first deal with their poverty and their hunger and their oppression, and then and only then can we expect them to be responsive to the things of the spirit. From such a viewpoint, could anything be more grotesque than the spectacle of a poor starved beaten wretch speaking to a group of poor starved beaten wretches about the relationship of the Immaculate to the persons of the Blessed Trinity? Yet their hearts were burning within them as they listened to his words.

Tyranny and injustice and oppression are evil things and we must do all in our power to drive them from the world. But experience has shown us that when one tyranny is driven out another all too often takes its place. This happens and will keep on happening as long as we think that liberation is a matter of political action and of that alone. True freedom does not come from a change of system but from a change of heart. The liberation offered by the Soviet army was a sad and deceptive thing compared to the liberation offered by prisoner no. 16670.

In Poland in 1971 I met Father Conrad Szweda. His memory of those days in Auschwitz thirty years earlier was still crystal clear. He summed up the message of Maximilian in these words:

> In that place love was, as it were, exterminated. In that place hatred and bitterness ruled. And yet, in these conditions, here was a man who stood up to defend love, to oppose hatred with love. Because of this love he gave his own life for another and this put us on our feet again and we said: Life is still worth living and hatred still hasn't got the last word.

> This I think was the greatest achievement of Father Kolbe: that he gave back their spirit and their strength to thousands — more than that, to tens of thousands — because they now began to believe in life, in the victory of truth and in the victory of love.